VERSATILITIES.

BY

R. H. NEWELL.

("ORPHEUS C. KERR.")

BOSTON:
LEE AND SHEPARD, PUBLISHERS.
NEW YORK:
LEE, SHEPARD, AND DILLINGHAM.
1871.

UNIVERSITY PRESS: WELCH, BIGELOW, & CO.,
CAMBRIDGE.

SEVERAL pieces of verse included in the graver half of the present collection were published some seven or eight years ago in a little volume, which, for private reasons, was almost immediately withdrawn from print. Of them, and of the greater number of "Poems" forming the first division of this book, the writer deems it unnecessary to say more, by way of introduction, than that they have all (with the exception of two or three self-betraying bits of youthful fancy) been unaffectedly spontaneous with him, — the inspirations of scenes, events, characters, sentiments, and intellectual conceptions specifically distinguishing themselves to his apprehension as presentments naturally demanding a poetic, rather than a prosaic, form of expression.

The "Satires and Burlesques" should possess the merit of amiability at least; for, while aimed chiefly at various superficialities and false pretensions in politics, literature, art, sentiment, and morals, their instigation has been, and is, principally the ludicrous, rather than the sinister, side of the subject satirized or burlesqued.

That the only popular humor of thought and personal character which is distinctively American, and that the particular imported humor which has become partially national with us by marked political and social adoption, seem to merit some illustration in commemorative rhyme, must be the placation of the æsthetical taste possibly taking exception to the character-sketches grouped under the forewarning caption of "Illiteraria."

With these brief preliminary notes the volume they introduce is submitted to the mercy of the friendly and the indifferent, by one who, having had the honor to experience the indulgence of the former in his prose, trusts that the title of his present venture may be esteemed sufficiently modest to exempt the latter from disturbance by his verse.

NEW YORK, April, 1871.

CONTENTS.

POEMS.

SATIRES AND BURLESQUES.

ILLITERARIA.

POEMS.

THE MOUNTAIN PATH.

FAR in a land where mighty mountain ranges
Sweep from the plain to pinnacles of mist;
Fires in the opal day's prismatic changes,
Shades in the night's star-broken amethyst;
Stood there a Youth with staff and bundle laden
Full in the path such pinnacles to scale,
And, at his side, a true and loving Maiden,
The fairest, fondest beauty of the vale.

White at their feet the village houses glimmer'd,
Simple of toil and eloquent of rest,
Bathed in the rays through vine and branches shimmer'd,
Seen from the height like eggs within a nest;—
Each to the eye, as came the looker's choosing,
Shell for the gentlest Dove that wooing flies,
Or, from its shelter, fitted but for loosing
A hardy, fearless Eaglet to the skies.

Up to the clouds, like World-creating fingers,
Reach'd from before the everlasting hills;
Stretch'd from the palm where warmth forever lingers,
Far to the tips where ice forever chills.

Thus, in the Hand of silent Nature reading
  Lines of the fates the minds of men command,
Thoughtful He stood, and, of the Maid unheeding,
  The winding, soaring, endless pathway scann'd.

Firm was his staff upon the stranded gravel,
  Straight was his form with rigidest intent,
Bright was his look with all the dream of travel
  Sleeping unpractised in a sentiment.
Scarce did he feel the arm upon his shoulder,
  Creeping by trembles to the softest yoke ;
Poised for the Heights his heart was growing colder,
  And shiv'ring, quiv'ring, feign'd the airy stroke.

She, with a face of wistful, mute appealing,
  Seeking, and fearful still, to meet his eye,
Knew not enough of guile to hide the feeling
  Born in a glance and dying in a sigh ;
Bound in her arms she sought to draw him to her,
  E'en as a mother wakes her child from sleep,
Using the fondest ways by which he knew her, —
  The wisest, sweetest wiles that women keep.

" Turn thee with me," she murmur'd, " for thou knowest" —
  Upon his cheek he felt her glowing breath —
" Full many trav'lers by the way thou goest
  Have but ascended higher unto Death.
Fair is the world, and wide enough extended
  To spare the foot from clambering its wall ;
Think, where the prints of human steps are ended,
  And solemn, awful Avalanches fall !

"See, where is curling in the vale below us
Smoke from the chimney of thy father's cot;
See, where the ones whose loving best should know us
Gaze from the roadside as they knew us not:
See, where the cattle thou and I have driven
Wait for our meeting at the wayside brook";—
Still like a statue, he, to whom was given
A trancing, yearning, breathless, Upward look.

"Turn thee with me unto our happy places,
Nor wish the lonely desert steep to dare;
Soar by the Love whose wing its idol raises
Nearer to Heaven at Home, than lifted there.
Turn thee with me; the twilight haze is falling
Thick from the summits like a warning spell;
Hark! from the hollow where to God is calling
The slowly swinging woodland chapel bell."

Still was his look upon the Path before him,
E'en as the look of Youth aspiring seems
When a too daring thought for sleep comes o'er him,
From the wild vision of his waking dreams!
Not for a moment sought his eye the glances,
Soft as the sun's first, tender morning streaks,
Brightly distilling dew to lave by chances
The mantling, fading roses of her cheeks.

Low was his voice, as one who only speaketh
That to his soul which no one else should hear;
Quick were his words, as one who, speaking, seeketh
Sounds from his thoughts to satisfy his ear.

Slowly her arms fell from him, like a garland
  Drooping its lilies to the swaying air ;
Chill'd like the heart that feels from others' far-land
  The bitter, wintry sense It is not there !

" Oft have I yearn'd thy solitudes to measure,
  Sons of the Mist and bearers to the sky ;
Light from thy loftiest brow that cuts the azure
  Tranceth my spirit like a sleepless Eye.
Grand were the joy from Height to Height to wander,
  New lands and seas o'erlook'd by ev'ry hill ;
Nor with a thought of tiring pause to ponder
  The farther, steeper, loftier summit still !

" Thrones of the Earth, to lift thy victor higher,
  Far, than the Kings who rule but acres told,
He that can prove thy hoariest peak's defier
  Stands a Supreme o'er all the Globe can hold.
Master of Thee, and with no steep before him
  Marking the limit of his strength's assail,
Then, with the Eagle, only, sweeping o'er him,
  The burning, deathless Stars shall bid him Hail !

" See ! where the sky descends thy brows to gather
  In the blue glories of its highest span ;
See ! where the clouds uplift their masses, rather
  Than, through their veil, thou less enticest Man.
Who, with a soul whose homage would become thee,
  Thinks of the storms from precipices hurl'd,
If, at the last, he view in transports from thee,
  The girdling, whirling Wonders of the World ! "

Then She again: "O blinded self-deceiver,
  And lost to thine own nature as thou art;
Be not thy brain in its own fire believer,
  The flame it feels is stolen from the heart!
Why unto Heights all desolate and lonely
  Go to behold the distant world before,
When the whole Universe repeateth only
  The nearer, clearer World around thy door?"

"Waves of the soul, that strand it in a heaven!" —
  Fix'd was his look, and passionate his tone —
"White with the rays from endless morning given,
  Ring'd with the flashing splendors of the Zone:
Crowns on thy crests in fadeless glory glisten,
  Bright as the orbs that round thy temples glow;
And to my ears there cometh as I listen
  An airy, silv'ry calling — and I go!"

Thus, each to each, the Youth and Maiden parted; —
  As birds that meet mid-air at hour of rest,
When one to soar aloft from sight has started,
  Leaving the other flutt'ring to the nest, —
And She went down into the valley vernal,
  To love, and toil with others, just the same,
And He went up where rear their heads eternal
  The snowy, lonely mountain-peaks of Fame!

PICCIOLA.

IT was a Sergeant old and gray,
  Well singed and bronzed from siege and pillage,
Went tramping in an army's wake,
  Along the turnpike of the village.

For days and nights the winding host
  Had through the little place been marching,
And ever loud the rustics cheer'd,
  'Till ev'ry throat was hoarse and parching.

The Squire and Farmer, maid and dame,
  All took the sight's electric stirring,
And hats were waved, and staves were sung,
  And kerchiefs white were countless whirring.

They only saw a gallant show
  Of heroes stalwart under banners,
And in the fierce heroic glow,
  'T was theirs to yield but wild hosannas.

The Sergeant heard the shrill hurrahs,
  Where he behind in step was keeping;
But glancing down beside the road,
  He saw a little maid sit weeping.

" And how is this ? " he gruffly said,
A moment pausing to regard her ; —
" Why weepest thou, my little chit ? " —
And then she only cried the harder.

" And how is this, my little chit ? "
The sturdy trooper straight repeated,
" When all the village cheers us on,
That thou, in tears, apart art seated ?

" We march two hundred thousand strong,
And that 's a sight, my baby beauty,
To quicken silence into song
And glorify the soldier's duty."

" It 's very, very grand, I know,"
The little maid gave soft replying ;
" And Father, Mother, Brother too,
All say ' Hurrah ' while I am crying ;

" But think — O Mr. Soldier, think,
How many little sisters' brothers
Are going all away to fight
And may be *kill'd*, as well as others ! "

" Why bless thee, child," the Sergeant said,
His brawny hand her curls caressing,
" 'T is left for little ones like thee
To find that War 's not all a blessing."

And " Bless thee ! " once again he cried ;
Then clear'd his throat and look'd indignant,

And march'd away with wrinkled brow
  To stop the struggling tear benignant.

And still the ringing shouts went up
  From doorway, thatch, and fields of tillage ;
The pall behind the standard seen
  By one alone of all the village.

The oak and cedar bend and writhe
  When roars the wind through gap and braken ;
But 't is the tenderest reed of all
  That trembles first when Earth is shaken.

ASPASIA.

UNDER the branches whose blossoms are fire,
  Gathering thrones in her glances —
Queen of the lilies that nod to the rose,
  Catching its color by chances ;
Treading a universe under her feet,
  Lo ! where the goddess advances.

Pearls are asleep in the waves of her hair,
  Gems on her bosom are dreaming ;
And from the smouldering worlds of her eyes
  Glories of ruin are gleaming —
Glories that glow from the ashes of hearts,
  With a smile over them beaming !

Rich is the fabric that falls to her feet,
  Rare are its labyrinth laces ;
Deep in their brightness the jewels her heart
  Throbs into meteor races,
Each in its beauty the torch of a grace,
  Lighting the temple of graces.

This is her Court in the Kingdom of Night,
  Princes are bending before her ;

Nobles and warriors wall her around,
  Ready to serve and adore her;
Even the sage breathes the incense of love
  Cast by her majesty o'er her.

Is she not sanctified? Mark how the priest,
  Heedless of all that he preaches,
Under the shallow disguise of the world
  Wooes her with silvery speeches!
He is a man, and the heart in his breast
  Lives on the lesson she teaches.

What is the sternness and strength of a man,
  Barbarous, monkish, or knightly,
When the Imperial Passion commands,
  Ruleth it ever so lightly?
Naught but a tottering wall of defence
  Rendering weakness unsightly!

Beauty may dwell in the statue of stone,
  As in the living Circassian;
But in the beautiful sculpture of God
  Is there what no man can fashion —
Life that is light bringing blindness to men,
  From the high altar of Passion.

Here is the priestess, and here is the queen,
  Fairest the light can illumine;
Worshipp'd by man in the highest estates
  Granted on earth to the human;
But to her altar and unto her throne
  Cometh no form of a woman.

Woe to the maiden, or mother, or wife,
  Tempted by pity to name her!
Even a thought of the sisterless one,
  Charity-given, would shame her;
Mothers may speak of the motherless one,
  Only to shudder and blame her.

She, by her mind, is too high for her sex —
  She, by her life, is below it;
And if the medium rests in her soul,
  Woman disdaineth to know it;
Charity, mark'd by a sneer of the world,
  Findeth no woman to show it!

She, in Philosophy's fathomless spring,
  Bathed her unsatisfied spirit;
Yearning for that which is not of the earth,
  Taking what seem'd to be near it,
Ere to her youth came the voice of the world,
  Warning her spirit to fear it.

(Life is a harp for the spirit to play,
  Given by God to his creature;
But by the pride that is virtue in man,
  Ruling his every feature,
All of its music is given to Art —
  None to the throbbings of Nature.)

By the FIRST IMPULSE she lives and is lost!
  Sacrificed unto the error,
That to the earliest good in the soul
  All the round world is a mirror;

Virtue the motive of ev'ry delight,
  Vice a perpetual terror.

Pure at the first, she were pure at the last,
  Had her mind's purity met her ;
But it was Falsehood, in Honor's disguise,
  That with illusions beset her,
Feigning a moment the truth of her soul,
  Only to rivet its fetter.

Think of her, then, in her womanless court,
  Maidens with sisters and mothers !
Think of her, lonely, with hundreds around,
  Maidens with fathers and brothers !
Think of her, truthful and pure in herself,
  Lost by the falsehood of others !

Under the branches whose blossoms are fire,
  Gathering thrones in her glances —
Queen of the lilies that nod to the rose,
  Catching its color by chances ;
Treading a universe under her feet,
  Lo ! where the goddess advances.

PSYCHE.

THY voice is in my dreams, O soul of love!
  Its soothing accents, murmuringly low,
Bend to no words, but musically flow
  In a fond influence; as the stars above
Syllable light, that would in sentence prove
  Bright as the Sun; yet is not e'en the Moon.

Thine eyes are, like the camel's, soft and clear,
  And deep with patience tenderly subdued,
As though an angel gazing through them view'd
  Vistas of Heaven mirror'd in the blear,
Glimmering waves, that from afar appear
  O'er the gray desert's solitary noon.

Thy touch is on my life; thy hands unseen,
  Blent with the glory shaded from thine eye
When thy soft glance steals upward to the sky
  Pleadingly, meekly — keep my spirit clean,
Banishing stains, or making them to mean
  Ashes from fire, or dust from purest air.

Thy form is ever with me, day and night;
  The city's crowds of evil and of good,

The cool, green chambers of the whisp'ring wood
   Holding thee near, impalpable to sight,
Silently close, a sanctity to light
   The tender Bible of a mother's pray'r.

Thy feet are on the path my heart would take,
   When weary, desolate, and sick of man,
It turns to where its youthful roadway ran
   Fairly to view, without a shape to break
Loneliness all ; yet, like a summer lake,
   Blithe with the dimpling dancers of the Sun.

I lean on thee for rest, as one who feels
   A heavy burden mocking at his strength,
And of his journey knoweth not the length,
   Nor where the ending ; but exhausted reels,
Pantingly weak, to where some turn reveals
   Stones of a grave to plant his staff upon.

I know thou art not dead, nor living thou,
   But borne an airy sculpture of the breath
Above the lilies motionless of death.
   So much the tomb hath marble from thy brow,
Veinless of pain, as life has lost but now
   Of the white innocence of perfect good.

O leave me not alone ; for losing thee,
   I lose the tender manliness of one
Who, lest some flow'r be hidden from the sun
   By his frail shadow cast upon the lea,
Thoughtfully turns to where his shade may be
   Lost in the rustling twilight of the wood.

My spirit clings to thee, and in its spells
  Of doubting all itself can worthy show
To hold thee steadfast, sadly come and go
  Fancies of ling'ring, fainting, far farewells,
Mournfully clear, as through a fog the bells
  Of some lost vessel sinking down at sea.

Still fondly bide with me; for thou art mine,
  As to myself a nobler self belongs,
The higher music dream'd in all my songs;
  What of my being might be half divine,
Rightfully grown, in Nature's first design;
  Not what I was, nor am, but what would be.

O keep me true to thee, that naught defile
  A truth unstudied to my fellow-man,
Plann'd for myself; as little children plan;
  Who, in their wisdom, selfish without guile,
Fancy the earth is happy when they smile,
  And think the world is drowning when they weep.

Nearer to thee I come, as o'er me roll
  The waved pulsations of ungrateful Wrong;
Though with my shadow moves my grave along —
  Nearer to thee for rest, as one whose goal
Forever is where ends his latest stroll,
  On his own shadow lays him down to sleep.

SPRING VIOLETS UNDER THE SNOW.

NOTHING is lost that has beauty to save,
Purity rises in flow'rs from the grave,
And from the blossoms that fade on the tree
Falleth the seed of the blossoms to be;
Life unto Death is mortality's growth,
Something immortal is under them both:
Surely as cometh the Winter, I know
There are Spring Violets under the snow.

See the old man in his great easy-chair,
Furrow'd his forehead and white is his hair:
Yet, as he roguishly smiles to his dame,
Pointing her eyes to the lovers, whose shame
Makes them withdraw from the light of the fire,
Boyhood, light-hearted, reveals in the sire!
Surely as cometh the Winter, I know
There are Spring Violets under the snow.

See the old wife, in her kerchief and cap,
Dropping her knitting-work into her lap,
While with a laugh that is silent she shakes,
And o'er her shoulder another peep takes:

Years are full fifty since she was miss,
Yet she 's a girl in that overheard kiss!
Surely as cometh the Winter, I know
There are Spring Violets under the snow.

See the Old People, with nods of delight,
Stealing together away for the night,
Ever too fond and too cunning to own
Why they should leave the shy lovers alone;
But their eyes, twinkling, are telling the truth—
Down in their hearts is an answering youth!
Surely as cometh the Winter, I know
There are Spring Violets under the snow.

LINCOLN.

I.

'TWAS needed — the name of a Martyr sublime,
To vindicate God in that terrible time!
'T was fitting the thunder of Heaven should roll,
Ere cannon exultant had deafen'd the soul
To what in all ages the Maker hath taught,
The pardon of Sin is with suffering bought.
And just was the doom that the lightning should fall
On him, the supreme and the head of us all,
Ere, blest in his living the triumph to seal,
The Victor forgot what the Brother should feel.
For still with the vanquish'd we shared in the guilt
That struck us at last to the murderous hilt;
And still unto us did the horror belong
Of helping a brother to wed with the Wrong,
'Till, foster'd to treason by parent and kin,
A Traitor to both was the child of the Sin.
Then thine to atone for the shame in the end,
Our gentle First Citizen, Chieftain, and Friend!

II.

And honestly plain as thyself be the verse
Such living and dying as thine to rehearse;

Not tuned to the rhythmical music of art,
But simple of note as the pulse of the heart
That answers the touch of the hand on the strings
When man for the noblest humanity sings.
From page unto page of thy story we trace
The strength of thy manhood, the light of thy face:
Thy merciful soul and thy wisdom are there,
An honesty open and clear as the air;
A spirit to mould from the fetters of birth
A crown for a peer of the kings of the earth;
A nature to wear in the palace of State
The mind of the humble that stand at the gate;
A grace, of humanity's brotherhood bred,
To bend with the wrong to the lowliest head;
To bear up the height unto freedom the Slave,
And find upon Pisgah his thanks — and a grave!

III.

How pure is the lustre of virtues that climb
Imperial summits of pow'r in their time,
Unaided by patronage, conquest, or birth,
But lifted aloft by the magic of worth:
Like jewels in primal reflection that shine, —
Not drawn from a casket, but raised from the mine,
A growth from the sunless domain of the moles,
Yet born with a splendor of light in their souls!
Behold where the boy at the plough in the West
Inherits such virtues to glow in his breast:
He knows not his riches; he bendeth to toil
Where scant is the harvest and stubborn the soil;
While broods in his bosom such patience serene
As giveth to labor its tenderest mien.

None tell to the liegeless of houses and lands
The fate of a people shall rest in his hands;
Yet sleeps there a might in the calm of his eye
To rescue a nation from death — and to die!

IV.

O, bitterest lot that the lowly can find,
Where labor's monotony crushes the mind,
Till poverty, prison'd in poverty still,
To dust is degraded, or madden'd to kill.
'T is thus in the countries far over the sea,
But happy the poor man, my Country, in thee;
For wide over thee may his industry range,
And sweeten his toil with the blessing of change.
From tracing the furrow and planting the grain,
The youth turneth back and forsaketh the plain:
He mates with the boatmen, and joins in their song,
Where rolleth the Father of Waters along:
Still patient with fortune, still earnest to bear
What God and humanity mark for his share.
None read from the future his glorious fate,
To stand at the helm of the vessel of State,
Its stay till the night and the tempest are done,
And then into Heaven go up with the sun!

V.

Well tried is the genius that rises to rule
From lessons of man in adversity's school:
Ill-balanced by honors too lavishly flung,
It scorneth the level from which it has sprung;

Imbitter'd by contest with rank as it rose,
Its texture is iron that hardens with blows;
Or, true to the balance, in victory mild,
It tow'rs like a mountain grown up from the wild;
Broad-set at its base in the primitive clod,
To shrink to a spire of the temples of God.
So he, in a grander simplicity hale,
Goes up to a height from obscurity's vale;
So, true to the lowly, sublime with the high,
To these he lends counsel, with those in his eye:
"Half Free and half Slave the Republic must fall;
Yet saved it shall be," are his words for us all!
Time put him to proof when the issue was tried —
He lived for the Deed, for the Principle died!

VI.

Now, borne on his countrymen's louder acclaim,
He mounts to the station most noble of fame;
A chief in the halls where a Washington stood,
And like unto him as the good to the good.
Foul Treason has risen, its horrors flame forth
To rouse from their slumbers the souls of the North,
And pealeth from cities, from prairies and farms,
The rallying cry of the loyal in arms.
War breaks on the Nation, she enters the strife
And struggles with traitors for Honor and Life!
Where dwelleth the spirit her being to save
From murderers bred in the toil of the slave?
The Capitol answers: the spirit is there,
And holdeth its court in the President's chair.

That nature so gentle containeth a will
Which glows like a fire in an air that is still. —
Alas! that our pillar of guidance by night
Should fade from the world at the coming of light!

VII.

Why follow the record? His glories are told
In all that his people the tenderest hold:
A nation redeem'd, and her banner unfurl'd
The fairest, the strongest, the best in the world.
Henceforth be that Banner to patriot eyes
A pray'r from its Shepherd of Stars in the skies, —
To plead that no judgment in malice may fall,
To speak for a charity free unto all,
To glow on the sword that is drawn for the Right,
While merciful still in the midst of the fight:
Henceforth be its legend for ages to view,
Its stripes of the dawn and its planeted blue,
That ere from its story the darkness was torn,
A something of Heaven shed blood on the morn,
In sign that 't is given the godlike of earth
To pass through a death for the millions' new birth, —
To die of the night's weary vigil and care,
When day the eternal first whitens the air.

ALONE.

THREE stalwart sons old Sweyn, the Saxon, had,
   Brave, hardy lads for battle or the chase;
And though, like peasant, barbarously clad,
   Each wore the Nameless Noble in his face:
One o'er another rose their heads in tiers,
Steps for their father's honorable years.

One night in Autumn sat they round the fire,
   In the rude cabin bountiful of Home;
Mild by the rev'rence due from child to sire,
   Bold in the manhood unto mast'ry come;
Working their tasks o'er huntsman's forest gear,
Loos'ning the bow and sharpening the spear.

Lost in his thoughts, old Sweyn, the Saxon, stood,
   Leaning in silence 'gainst the chimney stone;
Staring unconscious at the blazing wood,
   Steep'd in the mood of mind he oft had known;
As an old tree whose stoutest branches shake,
Scarce from their vigor sign of life will take.

Athol, the bearded, with his bow had done,
   Alfred, the nimble, laid his spear aside,

Edric, the fairest, tiring of his fun,
  Left the old hound to slumber on his hide;
Yet was their sire like one whose features seem
Shaded by sleep, and all their light a dream.

Bold in the favor of the eldest born,
  Athol, for both his younger brothers, spoke:
" Father, the fox is prowling in the corn,
  And hear the night-owl hooting from the oak;
Let us to couch." But Sweyn had raised his head,
And thus, unwitting what had pass'd, he said:—

" See, from my breast I draw this chain of gold,"—
  Fair in the firelight royally it shone,—
" This for his honor that shall best unfold
  Who, of all creatures, is the most Alone;
Take him from palace, monast'ry, or cot,
Loving unloved, forgetting, or forgot."

Then Athol spoke, with thoughtful tone and look:
  " He is the loneliest — most Alone of all,
Who, in a skiff to the mid-seas forsook,
  Finds not an echo, even, to his call;
If Echo lived, not all Alone were he;
But there 's no echo on the solemn Sea!"

And Alfred next:—" But lonelier, brother, far,
  The wretch that flies a just avenging rod.
To him all scenes are wastes, a foe the star,
  All earth he 's lost, yet knows no heav'n, no God;
Most Lonely he, who, making man his foe,
Unto man's Maker dareth not to go!"

Thus spoke the lads, with wit beyond their years ;
  And yet the old man held his beard and sigh'd,
As one who gains the form his wishing wears,
  But misses still a something most denied ;
Upon his youngest eager looks he turn'd,
And Edric's cheek with grace ingenùous burn'd.

" I think, my father," — and his tones were low, —
  " That lonelier yet, and most Alone, is he,
Scarce taught, though crowds are leading, where to go,
  And one face missing can no other see ;
Though all the Norman's court around him moves,
He is Alone apart from Her he loves."

A hush fell on them. Then, with loving air
  And all the touching romance of the Old,
The hoary father kiss'd young Edric's hair,
  And o'er his shoulders threw the chain of gold ;
Then fell upon his darling's neck and cried :
" I have been Lonely since thy Mother died ! "

A RUSSIAN LEGEND.

'TWAS night, dead night in the frozen North,
  Where the weird Aurora gleams
On the crystal course of the snow-white horse
  Of the god of sleepless dreams ;
And the light of the stars, in glassy bars,
  Was cold as the dead eye seems.

The air was thick with the deadly breath
  Of the Arctic iceberg-king,
That falls like a blight of a winter's night,
  In a tight'ning, freezing ring
On the throbbing brow and the heart below
  Of the mortal perishing.

'Twas night, dead night, and the village lights
  Were gone, like ghosts, in the gloom
That midnight fill'd with the silence chill'd
  Of an open, trackless tomb ;
But a skater stood on a frozen flood,
  Still-born in the ocean's womb.

His head to the misty East he bent,
  And peer'd in the distance far,

Like one who sought, or an instant caught,
  The ray of a guiding star ;
Then spurn'd with a heel of flashing steel
  The path of the whirlwind's car.

And swift as a shaft from bowstring sped,
  He flew with a noiseless speed ;
And the blushing flights of the Northern Lights
  Shook down the blazing seed
Of rainbows spread o'er the river dead ;
  But the skater took no heed.

His eyes were set in a ghastly stare
  At the gate of an unborn day,
And the sparks flew back in his shining track,
  As he sped to the East away,
And little he reck'd though the rainbows fleck'd
  The ice in a prismal spray.

" I come, my love, on the wind ! " he cried,
  " And swift must the sea-bird be
That reaches the nest of the mate loved best
  In his crag beside the sea,
Before I can kiss, with a bridegroom's bliss,
  The cheek that is pale for me.

" I 've sworn it, too, o'er the bridal wine,
  To ride on my steeds of steel
Far over the tide, to my maiden's side,
  Ere dawn shall the East reveal ;
And lo ! I defy all of earth or sky
  To fetter my wingéd heel ! "

He spoke : a blast came out of the North
  With mystic and whisp'ring sound ;
It struck like a knife to the skater's life,
  And his impious lips it bound
In a living death, that his smoking breath
  In vain might linger around.

And a stiff'ning film was in his eyes,
  And an adamantine band
Crept round his heart, with a deaden'd smart,
  And held it numbly spann'd ;
And the skater felt, on his shoulder-belt,
  The grasp of an icy hand !

A fearful voice from the blast came out —
  " Now, skater, away, away !
On a steed of steel, with a wingéd heel,
  Before 't is the break of day,
Where a bride now waits for the ring of skates,
  And where she may wait for aye !

" Then ride ! then ride ! thou skater bold,
  Who fear not the Earth nor Sky ;
And the hand of the strong shall urge along
  Till the tempests slower fly ;
But before thy pace shall have won the race
  The bride who waits may die ! "

Then swift as flash from the eye of storms,
  And swift as the leap of thought,
The skater he sped o'er the river dead,
  To the shadows, strangely wrought,

Of the mountains grim, where the spectres dim
   Have their revels often sought.

He felt that his blood was clogging fast,
   And his limbs grew stiff and chill ;
But the viewless hand, on his shoulder-band,
   Kept pressing him onward still !
And he knew, for his crime, through endless time
   'T would press, but it would not kill !

The river led to the frozen sea,
   The sea unto seas did run ;
And the hand press'd on when the night was gone,
   Nor ceased when the day was done ;
And the skater flew from the land he knew
   To a land without a sun.

No more from thence to return again
   To the lonely waiting bride,
Where she wept and pray'd for the lover stray'd
   From a heart so true and tried ;
And then, when the year to its end was near,
   Like a lily broken died.

THE WORLD'S HISTORY.

A BABY smiling on a mother's knee,
A faint ray breaking o'er an Eastern sea,
A green leaf peeping from a root deep set,
A candle waxen, and unlighted yet.

A school-boy mimicking a lark's clear cry,
A red flush blazoning a morning sky,
A frail twig bending to a zephyr's thought,
A candle twinkling with a spark just caught.

A lover kneeling to a maiden fair,
A sun all golden in a cloudless air,
A bud slow swelling on a fragrant bough,
A candle crested with a white flame now.

A soldier fighting for a prize ne'er gained,
A spot of fever on a zenith stain'd,
A branch low drooping with a fruit half sear,
A candle gutt'ring with a jaundiced blear.

A miser gloating at a coffer's brim,
A gray gleam ending in a twilight dim,
A dry leaf crackling in a wintry fall,
A candle smoking to a shadow'd wall.

A dotard gasping in a parson's ear,
A pale star dying in a storm-cloud near,
A tall tree loosening a clasp'd root-hand,
A candle flick'ring at a wick's last strand.

A shadow resting on a square of white,
A sun's ghost walking in a noon of night,
A prone trunk hollow to a worm's vile tread,
A candle wasted and a mortal dead.

THE PERFECT HUSBAND.

AS Light unto the Morn,
  So Time to him unfolds her;
As holds the day the light,
  So unto him he holds her.
A fairer than himself,
  To crown his manhood given,
A something less of earth —
  A something more of Heaven.

He deems her not a Saint —
  In loving she is human —
And as he is a Man,
  The dearer she as Woman.
Not down on her he looks,
  Nor up to an Ideal,
But straight into her eyes,
  And all his love is real.

As bends the sturdy tree
  To shade a pool of water,
But standeth like a rock
  When wind and torrent slaughter;

So bends he unto her
  When gentlest her controlling,
So stands he as a wall
  When dangers round are rolling.

'T is not by given Right,
  Or Privilege, he rules her;
For 't is his grace to yield,
  That in obeying schools her;
And if the less himself
  From troublous cause, or other,
A sharing Sister she,
  And he a patient Brother.

As she may have a fault,
  So he may have a greater,
And sorrow for his own
  For both is expiator;
And if upon her sleeve
  She snares a passing folly,
He frights it with a smile,
  And not with melancholy.

He slaves her truth to him
  By no confining portal,
But in himself reflects
  Its counterpart immortal.
The freedom that he gives
  Is taken from the donor:
A Husband's faith may rest
  Upon a Husband's honor.

2 *

And ever as a child,
  When childish she, he chides her,
And ever as a man,
  When she is strong, he guides her:
Through sunshine and through shade,
  Through blessing and disaster,
In more than name, her Friend,
  In less than law, her Master.

THE CONSECRATION.

THE woodlands caught the airy fire upon their
vernal plumes,
And echo'd back the waterfall's exultant, trilling
laugh ;
And through the branches fell the light, in slender
golden blooms.
To write upon the sylvan stream the Naiad's epitaph.

On either side the sleeping vale the mountains swell'd
away,
Each, bred of Nature's lore, a grand and solitary sage ;
And brightly in the teeming plain the river went astray,
Like an exhaustless vein of Youth wound through
a green Old Age.

The turtle woo'd his gentle mate, where thickest hung
the boughs,
While round them fell the blossoms pluck'd by
robins' wanton bills ;
And on its wings the zephyr caught the music of his
vows,
To waft a strain responsive to the chorus of the
hills.

'T was in a nook beside the stream where grapes in clusters fell,
And 'twixt the trees the swaying vines were lost in leafy show'rs,
That fauns and satyrs, tamed to rest beneath the noon-day spell,
Gave silent ear and witness to the meeting of the flow'rs.

The glories of the fields were there in summer's bright array,
The virgins of the temple vast where Noon to Ev'ning nods,
To crown as queen of all the rest whose bosom should display
The signet of a mission blest, the cipher of the gods.

The royal Lily's sceptred cup besought an airy lip,
The Rose's stooping coyness told the bee was at her heart,
While all the other sisters round, with many a dainty dip,
Sought jewels hidden in the grass, and waved its spears apart.

"We seek a queen," the Lily said, "and she shall wear the crown
Who to the Mission of the Blest the fairest right shall prove;
For unto her, whoe'er she be, has come in sunlight down
The badge of Nature's Royalty, from angel hands above.

"I go to deck the wreath that binds a fair, imperial brow,
Whose whiteness shall not be the less that mine is purer still;
For though a band of sparkling gems is set upon it now,
'T will be the fairer that the Church in me beholds her will."

"I claim a loyal suitor's touch," the Rose ingenuous said,
"And he will choose me when he seeks the bow'r of lady fair,
To match me, with a smile, against her cheek's betraying red,
And place me, with a kiss, within the shadows of her hair."

And next the proud Camellia spoke: "Where festal music swells,
And solemn priest, with gown and book, a knot eternal ties,
I go to hold the veil of her who hears her marriage-bells,
And pledges all her life unto the Love that never dies."

The Laurels raised their glowing heads, and into language broke:
"'T is ours to honor gallant deeds that awe a crouching world;
We rest upon the warrior's helm when fades the battle's smoke,
And bloom perennial on the shield that back the foeman hurl'd."

And other sisters of the field, the woodland, and the vale,
Each told the story of her work, and glorified her quest;
But none of all the noble ones had yet reveal'd the tale,
That taught them from the gods she wore the signet in her breast.

At length the zephyr raised a leaf, the lowliest of the low,
And there, behold a Violet the Spring let careless slip;
Beyond its season blooming there where newer beauties grow,
Enshrined like an immortal thought that lives beyond the lip.

"We greet thy presence, little one," the graceful Lily said,
And quiver'd with a silent laugh behind her snowy screen,
"Upraise unto the open sun thy modest little head;
For here, perchance, in thee at last the Flow'rs have found their queen."

A tremor shook the timid flow'r, and soft her answer came;
"'T is but a simple duty left to one so small as I;
And yet I would not yield it up for all the higher fame
Of nodding on a hero's helm, or catching beauty's eye.

"I go to where an humble mound uprises in a field,
With not a sculptured line to mark the lonely sleeper's name;
Where, in the solitude of death, the sacrifice is seal'd,
That made a solitude of life to bear another's blame.

"I go to blossom o'er the heart that felt the scorn of men
While breaking, in its patient love, a brother-man to save;
To die of wintry cold, as he, and with the Spring again
To blossom," said the Violet, "upon his friendless grave."

There fell a hush on all the flow'rs; but from a distant grove
Burst forth the anthem of the birds in one grand peal of praise;
As though the stern old Forest's heart had found its early love,
And all of earth's sublimity were melted in its lays!

Then, as the modest flow'r upturn'd her blue eye to the sun,
There fell a dew-drop on her breast, as shaken from a tree;
The lowliest of the sisterhood the godlike Crown had won;
For hers it was to consecrate Truth's Immortality.

The woodlands caught the airy fire upon their vernal
plumes,
And echo'd back the waterfall's exultant, trilling
laugh;
And through the branches fell the light, in slender
golden blooms,
To glorify the Violet, the Nameless Epitaph.

THE MADMAN.

GO count the glimm'ring lanterns of the sky,
And be thou priest of all their mystic rites;
That when the world shall ask — What makes them fly
Through boundless space, nor blend with other lights?
Thy tongue, with subtlety, may show their flights
To be obedient to a set of rules
Laid down by learned men, who make the nights
Their hours of study, and do teach in schools
That ancient scholars were less wise than modern fools.

Mark well the current of a woman's thought,
When, on his knees, the master of her heart
Pleads, with the eloquence his love hath taught,
For one short word; and see her quickly start,
As though 't were unexpected on her part;
And see her shun the form she longs to press,
And see her practise a defiant art —
Then tell me, if the riddle thou canst guess,
Why says she falsely "No," while her fond heart says "Yes"?

But who can read the human mind, and tell
How all its qualities should order'd be?

And how arranged, its secret springs work well,
And how, disorder'd by insanity?
O, who shall justify the vanity
Of those who boast of reason, and will show
That, in the system of humanity,
The mind is darken'd, when it does not glow
With the reflected light of other minds below?

I 've seen a madman; and they call'd him so
Because he scorn'd the ways of other men;
Yet, as he walks his dungeon to and fro,
His pride is like the lion's in his den;
And you would style them prince and subject when
His jailor enters, to inquire of him
If he has any orders there and then,
Which, being answer'd, may assuage his whim?
But you shall hear how I did chance to meet with him.

'T was in a madhouse! Do not start, good friend, —
I am not mad, nor even like to be
(Though there are many people who pretend
That I am crazed, because my words are free).
I only went to visit; just to see
How the poor maniac differ'd from the man
Of Reason; and how his philosophy
Went roving from the nicely order'd plan
That Custom dictates, since its potent reign began.

The keeper was a jolly fellow, born
With a broad, stationary laugh upon his face,
That age to countless wrinkles deep had worn;

And, as he guided me about the place,
He jested oft, and with a homely grace,
Upon the creatures held in bondage there;
And dwelt upon the evils of his race,
With such a laughing and triumphant air,
That one might almost think he gloried in despair.

"Yonder," said he, "you see that female dress'd
In bits of carpet, and a crimson skirt?
Well, she was once with twenty lovers blest,
But — would you b'lieve me? — the confounded flirt
Just play'd with all, until their hearts were hurt,
And then she sent them sighing from her side,
And told the story in a manner pert;
But, sir, she spoil'd her chance to be a bride —
And here she is at last, and here will she abide.

"That fellow was a poet, and I hear
He wrote good verses — or, at least, 't is clear
He thought so — but some surly critic's sneer
Sent him to Boston first; then he came here.
O, you should hear him talk of 'Jenny, dear,'
And all the orange-blossoms in her hair,
And how he honestly believes her tear
To be a dew-drop, fragrant, and as fair
As ever 'took its flight' through 'Eden's' — something
— 'air.'

"Here 's an old maid. — Law, Betty, don't be mad
(But she *is* mad, sir, as a hare in March),
I 'm sure this single gentleman is glad
To meet a lady graceful as a larch.

Ah, sir! (aside) for all she looks so arch,
She is as crazy as a bug in bed;
And daily covers all her head with starch,
Because she fancies that her hair is red.
Poor thing! she 's only mad because she cannot wed.

"And there 's a lawyer — such a lively chap! —
Who 's always arguing some mighty 'cause';
And sometimes takes that dog upon his lap,
And talks to it about the 'Statute Laws,'
As though the animal, instead of paws,
Had hands to furnish an enormous fee;
Or, as a pris'ner, long'd to find some clause
That might entitle him to liberty.
O, he 's the strangest man — and mad as mad can be!

"But here 's the wildest madman of them all —
You see we have to bind him with a chain.
He has a notion that the sky would fall
If he, as Emperor, should cease to reign;
In fact, sir, he is hopelessly insane,
And raves so strangely, in his frantic way,
That all attempts to quiet him are vain
Until the fit has left him for the day.
Just speak to him, good sir, and see what he will say."

A wreck of manhood stood within a cell,
Where endless night with the inconstant morn
For mast'ry strove; and from his waist there fell
An iron chain, that in his writhes had torn
Great, gaping wounds, and on his limbs had worn

The brand of infamy — a felon's brand.
His robe was rags, his beard was all unshorn,
And like a vulture's talon was his hand —
Yet proud as king of countless kingdoms did he stand!

"Why are you here?" respectfully I said;
For there was something in his aspect then —
A crown of nature on his fallen head —
That gave the fetter'd madman in his den
An air superior to common men.
I felt as they who ruin'd temples see,
And own the influence of past ages, when
Each pillar tower'd in matchless symmetry,
And ev'ry hall echo'd the tread of royalty!

The madman heard me with a nervous start,
And glared upon me with his blazing eyes,
Then placed a wither'd hand upon his heart
(Or where the heart of reasoning people lies),
As one tormented with strange terror tries
To close his bosom 'gainst a full belief
Of some dread woe that on a rumor flies —
And, in his fear, scarce comprehends his grief.
Thus stood that human wreck upon misfortune's reef.

"Why came I here!" he said; while from his lips
The froth went streaming o'er his matted beard,
And thence upon his breast: "Why come the ships
Unto their ports? Because by MAN they're steer'd.
I am a ship; and when I boldly veer'd
From Custom's pathway and his common home,
Men seized my vital tiller, loudly jeer'd,

And to the port of madness made me come!
But I defy them all — King, Kaiser, Pope of Rome!"

"He raves!" the keeper whisper'd. "Let us go!"
"Not yet," I answer'd; for a mystic spell
Was stealing o'er my senses; and the woe
Of him before me in that dreary cell
Was like the shadowy waters of a well
Wherein I saw familiar features, fraught
With the strange meaning of an hour when fell
A midnight blackness on my world of thought,
And all my inmost soul its dark contagion caught.

"Tell me the tale," I mutter'd, in a tone
So deep in its intensity, and wild,
That I did scarcely know it for my own.
And then the madman shook his head and smiled—
But such a smile! It was of mirth defiled
With the new traces of a thousand tears, —
Each tear of some dread agony the child, —
A smile that Death in ghastly triumph wears;
One gleam of wrinkled light upon a storm of years!

"Hear me!" he shouted. "Hear the wondrous tale
That might confound a chicken-hearted slave,
And make him shudder, and his cheek turn pale;
But if, like me, thou dost not fear to brave
A world of fools, nor findest in each grave
A ghost to haunt thee in its winding-sheet,
Thou shalt exult with me when I do rave,
And glory in the wonders I repeat;
For we are man and man — in sympathy we meet!

"I loved a maiden once, — a gentle girl,
Bred in a valley where the sloping hills
Reflect each other's beauties. Like a pearl,
In a rude shell, I found her; and the rills
That mock the birds of summer with their trills
Were not more pure, more fresh, more bright than
she.
Hers was a beauty that the bosom thrills
With the love-notes of its own ecstasy;
And her fond guileless heart knew me, and only me!

"We stood before the altar at the hour
When all the west is planted thick with light,
And ev'ry cloud is bursting into flow'r,
And blooms amid the banners of the night.
We wedded, and I left her; for the sight
Of her sweet blushes so o'ercharged my soul
With wondrous joy, that I was madden'd quite,
And in my madness could not brook control;
Man knew not half my bliss — God, only, knew the
whole!

"I wander'd in the fields, yet saw no earth,
Nor sun, nor sky; for I was in a dream
That gave unto another world a birth.
O God! had this world been as that did seem!
But I awoke, to find the subtle beam
Of madness fled. I had been dreaming long;
But Reason seized again the rule supreme,
And as she checked fond Love's delusive song,
My guilty soul was conscious of a heavy wrong!

" I sought my bride again. She smiled on me,
And placed her little hands within my own,
And kiss'd my forehead so confidingly,
That I could scarce repress the rising groan.
O God! Why had I not a heart of stone,
To save her blessed spirit from the taint
Of selfish love, that, in its wild desire,
Would see the mortal only in the saint,
And make a pretext of its holy fire?
But I wash'd out my guilt — the sacrifice was dire!

" They led her to her couch, and when I sought
The old oak chamber, at a later hour,
Angels of slumber o'er her soul had wrought
The subtle influence of their gentle pow'r
And woven dreams. The minutes that devour
The night were nearing Twelve; above the hill
The moon swept slowly, and her silver show'r
Stream'd softly, coldly, o'er the window-sill;
Tired Nature slept in peace, and all was hush'd and
still.

" With noiseless step, I cross'd the chamber floor,
Drew the pale curtains of the couch aside,
And, like a troubled spirit on the shore
Of a lost Heav'n, I look'd upon my bride.
O, she was beautiful! and, in the pride
Of fearless innocence, she calmly slept,
Like rosebud on a lily open'd wide;
And, as a dream-laugh o'er her features crept,
The fountain of my tears flow'd over, and I wept!

" But as I wept, I saw a bitter sneer
Drawn with a moonbeam on a spectral face
Press'd close against the glass. 'Fool! dost thou fear
To rise superior to thy coward race?'
A taunting echo rang about the place,
And my great purpose was revived again
'I do not fear!' I cried. 'God grant me grace
To yield to thee a soul without a stain;
She came unstain'd to me, and spotless shall remain!'

" I bent above her, and she gave a start —
Like one affrighted — softly breathed my name,
Then slumber'd on. Then I did act a part
That might eclipse a Christian martyr's fame,
And make the laurell'd hero blush for shame;
Down through the snowy temple of the soul
I struck the glitt'ring blade, and quench'd the flame
Of a young life, that all the brightness stole
From my own martyr'd heart, as the red drops did roll!

" They call'd me MADMAN for it, fetter'd me,
And shut me in a prison — where I stand
To bear the bitter mockings of the free,
And live a by-word for a darken'd land!
Virginius slew his *child* with his own hand,
To save her from a tyrant; I did slay
My *bride* to save her from *myself!* How grand
The deed! Yet worlds their lasting homage pay
Unto the Roman HERO — but I 'm MAD, they say!"

The madman paused, and turn'd away his face —
As though he would not have a stranger know
That he could weep. Then, with the haughty grace
Of one to empire born, he bade me go
Forth from his royal presence ! Bowing low,
I left him in his solitary den
To weep, and rave, and live, and die, as though
He to the world unknown had ever been,
And, being curs'd of God, was doubly curs'd of men !

DOLCE FAR NIENTE.

I.

STILL as a fly in amber hangs the world,
In a transparent sphere of golden hours,
With not enough of life in all the air
To stir the shadows or to move the flow'rs;
And in the halo broods the angel Sleep,
Woo'd from the bosom of the midnight deep
By her sweet sister Silence, wed to Noon.

II.

Held in a soft suspense of summer light,
The gen'rous fields with all their bloom of wealth
Bask in a dream of Plenty for the years,
And breathe the languor of untroubled Health.
Without a ripple stands the yellow wheat,
Like the Broad Seal of God upon the sheet
Where Labor's signature appeareth soon.

III.

As printed staves of thankful Nature's hymn,
The fence of rails a soothing grace devotes,
With clinging vines for bass and treble clefs,
And wrens and robins here and there for notes; —

Spread out in bars, at equal distance met,
As though the whole bright summer scene were set
To the unutter'd melody of Rest!

IV.

Along the hill in light voluptuous wrapt
The daisy droops amid the staring grass,
And on the plain the rose and lily wait
For Flora's whispers, that no longer pass;
While in the shade the violet of blue
Finds in the stillness reigning nature through,
That which her gentle modesty loves best.

V.

The mill-wheel motionless o'ershades the pool,
In whose frail crystal cups its circle dips;
The stream, slow curling, wanders in the sun,
And drains his kisses with its silver lips;
The birch canoe upon its shadow lies,
The pike's last bubble on the water dies,
The water-lily sleeps upon her glass.

VI.

Here let me linger, in that waking sleep
Whose dreams are all untinged with haunting dread
Of Morning's finger on the eyelids press'd,
To rouse the soul and leave the vision dead.
And while deep sunk in this soft ecstasy
I count the pulse of Heaven dreamily,
Let all life's bitterness behind me pass!

VII.

How still each leaf of my oak canopy,
That holds a forest syllable at heart,
Yet cannot stir enough in all its veins
To give the murmur'd woodland sentence start!
So still — so still all nature far and near,
As though the world had check'd its breath to hear
An angel's message from the distant skies!

VIII.

This one last glance at earth — one, only one —
To see, as through a veil, the gentle face
Bent o'er me softly, with a timid love
That half distrusts the sleep which gives it grace.
The thought that bids mine eyelids half unclose
Fades to a dream, and out from Summer goes,
In the brown Autumn of her drooping eyes.

OUR GUIDING STARS.

TO loud huzzas our Flag ascends,
  As climbs a flame the dizzy mast,
Till all its burning glory bends
  From where the azure seals it fast ;

And, pliant to the chainless winds,
  A blazing sheet, a lurid scroll,
The Compact of the Stars it binds,
  In fire that warms a nation's soul!

The planets of its field are set
  In God's eternal blue sublime,
Creation's world-wide starry stripe
  Between the banner'd days of time.

Upon the sky's divining roll,
  In burning punctuation borne,
They shape the sentence of the night
  That prophesies a cloudless morn.

The waters free their mirrors are ;
  And fair with equal light they look
Upon the royal ocean's breast,
  And on the humble mountain brook.

Though each distinctive as the soul
  Of some new world not yet begun,
In bright career their courses blend
  Round Liberty's unchanging Sun.

Thus ever shine, ye Stars, for all!
  And palsied be the hand that harms
Earth's pleading signal to the skies,
  And Heav'n's immortal Coat of Arms.

A SONG FOR THE UNSUNG.

NOT often man's nature revealeth in tears
The springs of affection o'ergrown with his years;
Not often the rock of his spirit will shrink
To yield what a world may be dying to drink;
Yet comes there to me, as it ever will come,
Enshrined in my dreams of the altar at home,
One face that I cry for — so sweet when it smiled! —
My Sister, my Sister, you make me a child.

As music that falls, with no singer to word,
As rain blessing earth when no thunder is heard,
As light that still lingers when set is the sun,
As soft sounds that echo through silence begun;
So cometh the trust of thy heart unto mine,
So answers my spirit the pleadings of thine;
So speak for us both to the witnessing skies,
My Sister, my Sister, thy worshipping eyes.

My friend and companion through years that are gone,
As gentle as twilight, as pure as the dawn,
The thought that 's an eagle while roaming world-free
Is turn'd to a dove when it nestles with thee;
And, folding its wings in thy beautiful truth,
Renews on thy bosom its passionless youth,

And blesses the hand ever soothing its rest —
My Sister, my Sister, my truest and best.

When parents grew stern that a child should annoy,
How fondly you pled for the passionate boy;
How patiently bearing what angels might fret,
To soothe me in sickness, I cannot forget.
My life has its record of good and of ill,
With those to applaud and to censure at will;
But ever where thine was the finger to trace,
My Sister, my Sister, how perfect the grace!

The friendship that rides on the wave of the world
Is mine while the sails of my bark are unfurl'd,
And wafts me along o'er a midsummer sea
To havens where Fortune sits waiting for me;
But O, should the tempest break over my head,
What hands would be lifted, what pray'r would be said,
To save from the last falling stroke of the rod?
My Sister, my Sister, thine only — to God.

O, call it not Love that I give unto thee;
For love, like a feverish sun on the sea,
Is only a blossom of light from the seed
Of stars that were sown when the night was in need;
A growth from the darkness to dwindle once more
And break into atoms, then bloom as before,
An endless unrest ever changing above, —
My Sister, my Sister, it cannot be Love.

But call it a name that if spoken in pray'r
Would waft no alloy of the earth through the air;

A name by an impulse of reverence giv'n
To something all fair with the beauty of Heav'n ;
A name whose soft incense of truth shall impart
A fragrance refined in the dews of the heart.
So pure is the feeling, though simple it be,
My Sister, my Sister, I give unto thee.

'T is sweet to remember the moments gone by,
When more was the pow'r in a glance of thine eye
To hold me from evil perverting the will,
Than blows, that in childhood a manhood may kill.
And if in the future my destiny turns
To paths where the thorn is the finger that spurns,
Though others may scorn what I seem unto them,
My Sister, my Sister, thou wilt not condemn.

For still, though I leave thee, thy spirit will shine
A Bethlehem Star o'er the journey of mine,
And lead it from perils where luxuries nod
To find in a manger the glory of God.
While burneth a planet that Star shall be there,
The rent in the heavens where enter'd a pray'r,
When kneeling at even' thy form I could see —
My Sister, my Sister, that pray'r was for me!

If aught to offend thee I do while I live,
Forgive me! forgive me! and God will forgive ;
Not His to withhold from the suppliant's cry,
While thine is the tenderness watching His eye.
And as I go down in the valley of death,
Once more but a child at his earliest breath,
My soul's dying impulse shall pause in its flight,
My Sister, my Sister, to bid thee Good Night.

THE PRISONER OF FORTRESS MONROE.

(1866.)

WHERE ramparts frown upon the waves
 That leap and crouch like hounds below,
And Ocean's hoary giant-slaves
 In sullen murmurs surge their woe,
 With face upon his hands he sits,
 With broken heart and wand'ring wits,
 And starts at ev'ry gleam that flits
From the sea at his window-sill:
For the sound in his ears is still
 Andersonville!
Andersonville is the word from the sea to him,
There in his cell, in the casemate lone and dim.

The sentry's step upon the walk
 He hears; but not as mortals hear;
And closer with it seems to stalk
 A ghastly thing from off a bier —
 A something ever near the door,
 To enter once, and then no more
 Be visitor upon the floor
Of the Man it is sent to kill!
And the thought comes quick and chill —
 Andersonville!

Andersonville is the shadow of Death to him,
There in his cell, in the casemate lone and dim.

Hour follows hour from morn till night,
  As grave on grave in silence creeps ;
And earth with Life's twin-brother wakes ;
  And earth with Death's twin-brother sleeps !
    And all in one dread horror blends,
    That ne'er commences, never ends ;
    But through his broken spirit send
With an awful and vengeful thrill,
That scene of his murderous will —
        Andersonville !
Andersonville is the vision of Time to him,
There in his cell, in the casemate lone and dim.

'Twixt fort and sky the banner glows ;
  And as the darkness wraps it round,
Its vague and stifled flutter grows
  The life-blood bubbling from a wound !
    There ! there ! again the creature cries
    For food ; and, mad with suff'ring, dies
    By his own hand before their eyes
Who have shared in his ev'ry ill,
And there they bend over him still —
        Andersonville !
Andersonville is the prison that maddens him,
There in his cell, in the casemate lone and dim.

The moon swims slowly o'er the walls,
  A damp, dead mirror of the sun ;

And where her light all pallid falls
  The waters colder seem to run ;
    It pierces through the dungeon grate,
    To make ten thousand forms of hate
    Grin ghastlier from each granite plate
That would armor him safe from ill !
And the hiss in his ear is shrill —
      Andersonville !
Andersonville is the dream of the night to him,
There in his cell, in the casemate lone and dim.

Along the billow sweeps the gull,
  Not lonely while she hears her wings ;
And, lonelier, in the vapor dull,
  The lark unsolitary sings.
    With face upon his hands he sits,
    With broken heart and wand'ring wits,
    And starts at ev'ry gleam that flits
From the sea at his window-sill ;
And the word to his soul is still
      Andersonville !
Andersonville is alone in the world with him,
There in his cell, in the casemate lone and dim !

COSMO-BELLA.

THE roseate Morning, with girdles of light,
Has lifted the hills from the wave of the night,
And crown'd with a halo, and mantled in gray,
Retires to the mist and gives birth to a day.

What bird shall be first from his covert to spring,
And o'er the nativity earliest sing?
What flow'r shall be first, in the valley below,
To breathe out her dew in the coronal glow?

No bird of the mountain, no rose of the vale,
Shall earliest carol and blush with the tale;
For soft, through the hush of God blessing the scene,
Come feathery footfalls, the steps of a queen.

She comes! and the purity lapt in the hour
Takes presence and form in the beauty her dow'r;
She stands at her mirror, a hill-dripping stream,
And all the round world sees her smile in a dream.

Search not through the lands, from the Poles to the
Zone,
In quest of the Beauty one nation may own;
For all the Globe's gifts of perfection appear
In Beauty's Ideal, the Innocence here.

The Sea hoards a gem, and the Sky garners rays,
The one is her soul, and the others her ways;
And Nature, adoring, beholds in her eyes
The blue of the sea in the light of the skies.

Her features, illumed with the star-beam of Peace,
Are lined to the Art-worshipp'd contour of Greece;
And England's red roses, that grew in her glance,
Are blent on her cheek with the lilies of France.

The bloom of Circassia, the grace of Cathay,
Her lips move to life and her form gives a sway;
And white gleams her bosom through shadows of lawn,
The snow of the Alps in the pearl of the dawn.

The first golden circle the Tyrol to light,
Thrown off like a ring from the finger of night,
Has crumbled to dust in a summery air,
And scatter'd a day in the folds of her hair.

She stands with one foot in a thought of advance,
A foot on the velvet of roses to dance;
And, jewell'd with glittering dew, is display'd
The high-arching instep of Switzerland's maid.

Proud Europe, soft Asia, and Africa far,
She gathers your beauties wherever they are,
And, wearing them modestly, blesses our sight,
The Daughter of Morning, an Angel of light.

DITHYRAMBUS.

(From the German.)

TRUST me forever,
Doubt me, love, never,
While the world rolls.
What though to-day may be dying in shadows?
Morning shall rainbow the mists on the meadows,
Aurora shall light them with souls!

Now swelleth the bosom
With rapturous feeling,
And Care is forgotten
In Heaven's revealing.
Worlds upon worlds for a moment like this,
With the lips stealing
Nectar that quickens and glows in a kiss!

Let the gods hear me!
Stay, ye gods, near me:
Heed ye my praise?
Lo! I extol, with a reverence trembling,
You, that to banish the spirit's dissembling
Open the heavenly spheres to my gaze.

Such ecstasy raises
Earth's bitterest sorrows
To glorified promise
Of rosy to-morrows;
Leading each heart through the sepulchre's night,
'Mid transports and revel,
Into Elysian temples of light.

Great gods, inspire me!
With the flame fire me
Meet for thy bard —
That he may soar to Olympus immortal,
With Charis, the smiling, embrace at the portal,
In Eros behold his reward!

I rise, I 'm ascending,
The world grows a clod;
With heaven I 'm blending,
The dream of a god!

BATTLE-NIGHT.

ON the far borders of the dimming world
Gleam the last brands of watch-fires, kindled when
The hosts of day, retreating, paused and furl'd
Their shining standard in the sea; and then,
Sullen and ready for the strife again,
Lit the cloud-cities of the yielded plain
To conflagration vengeful; mocking men
With the flame-eaten palace, arch and fane,
Of whose red grandeur, now, but smould'ring clouds remain.

Already creep the stealthy scouts of Night
Along the shadows by the Ocean cast,
With Midnight at its heart, against the height
Where broods th' eternal Mother of the Vast:
Each veil'd in coming dreams of what is past —
Yet dropping from their mantles, as they crawl,
Bright, virgin jewels, polish'd by the blast,
And marking out in kingdoms, where they fall,
A sleep-reflected heritage for one — for all.

Alas! the drowsy lids of yesterday
Closed on a scene, that, like a bosom fair,

Was fit to gather down such Peace, and pray
That it might never garner less of care;
But now, the dead day's ashes in the air
Melt through a tainted twilight on the field,
Where Peace sits mourning, with dishevell'd hair
And blood-shot eyes, o'er Mercy's broken shield —
Peace made the slave of War; Mercy, of Death the yield!

Through the new eve like a disorder'd pall
Stretches the broken ground, with awful lines
Of human shape in ev'ry rise and fall;
Here, the bow'd head in dreadful sleep reclines;
There, a stout arm with other arms intwines;
And, yonder, mark the semblance of a form
Twisted and wrench'd in all the mad designs
Of a young tree, made jester to the storm:
Ice to the touch, that hand — 't will ne'er again warm!

Thousands on thousands, far and near they lie,
Lover and foe, pursuer and pursued, —
Some with glazed eyeballs, glaring at the sky,
And some — as though with sudden grief imbued
By the last scene their eyes in dying view'd —
Prone with their ghastly faces to the earth;
And some, with life's grim smile in death renew'd,
In the death-stare immortalizing mirth.
O age without a soul, to give such horrors birth!

Yonder the battery, all shatter'd, lies;
And here the drum, by some wild weapon torn;

And ev'rywhere the charger, half in rise,
Puts the poor dignity of man to scorn
And blends his blood with that of noblest born.
Join'd in the grim democracy of war,
Rider and horse, soldier, and sword once worn,
Find no degrees when the fierce battle o'er
Leaves them in equal graves — slain, broken, used no more.

The burly Guardsman, at his captain's feet,
Still the bent musket holds, with iron grip,
As though more eager yet the foe to meet —
Because blood gloves the hand upon his hip;
And, in the rigid tension of his lip,
Lurks the one sentence God alone may speak.
Soldier, thy bravery hath made a slip,
And borne thee with it where no foemen seek
To test the strength once thine — the strength now less than weak.

And thou, poor Stripling! with the girlish hair,
And hand so white around the pond'rous hilt,
It seems like Beauty, taken in a snare, —
What dost thou here, with death around thee built
In such close prison, for the Nation's guilt?
O, for a mother's hope — a sister's dream —
That died in darkness, when the blood was spilt
In whose warm current dwelt the living beam
God made to brighten Age, with its own youth's redeem.

Gone are the conq'ring banners of the day —
Hush'd the grand roar of the artillery —

And perish'd all the pomp and brave display
That mask'd the Battle in mad revelry!
Gone is the smoke that hid the battery;
And of the with'ring lightning-fire that bloom'd
Upon a field of bayonets for thee,
And mark'd thee, Soldier, with the ones it doom'd,
These ashes poor remain — to blend, to be entomb'd.

Draw, gentle Night, thy curtains closer round,
And fly, ye clouds, to hide the rising moon
From the white faces staring from the ground.
The morning light will come, alas! too soon,
That its fair beam must cancel all the boon
Of countless hearts, to whom the Night is hope
For blest escape of loved ones, who, at noon,
Reel'd in the charge, and fell upon the slope.
Leave them one feeble stay, with their despair to cope.

To-morrow all the land, from North to South,
May ring with echoes of a Battle won;
The rose may blossom at the cannon's mouth,
And trumpet honors unto Peace be done;
But, from his ramparts, will the rising Sun
See where the carrion crows expectant flit;
And while to crown her, worlds have just begun,
The Nation, sick at heart rememb'ring it,
Shall, at her lonely hearth, in dust and ashes sit.

SUMMER.

THE fickle year is in its golden prime;
  The world is dreaming in a hazy lustre,
And round the altars of our Summer clime,
  The blushing roses cluster.

Upon the mountain dwells impassion'd light,
  And in the valley sleeps a shade depressing,
While fields of waving wealth enchant the sight,
  Like gold of God's own blessing.

The ploughman rests beneath the wayside tree,
  The stream curls slowly round the hoofs of cattle;
And o'er the meadow floats the droning bee,
  Fresh from his flow'ry battle.

Soft through the Southern meshes of the vine,
  I hear the birds unto each other calling;
And in the casket of the eglantine
  The tropic dews are falling.

Far in the distance rolls the sluggish sea,
  With not enough of life in all its breathing
To bid the sail from its rude bonds go free,
  And spurn its hempen wreathing.

On all there rests a halo and a hush,
  The spell of poesy is on the blossom,
And Nature's spirit slumbers in a blush,
  Caught from high Heaven's bosom.

The Past and Future blend in one sweet sleep,
  The world 's a dream, and Care a hidden mummer,
Whose tears, however sadly he may weep,
  Are but the dews of Summer.

THE GENERAL'S WIFE.

SHE hears the thunder of his guns
  Deep-crashing o'er the lowland farms,
And all the ardor of her soul
  Goes forth to greet her lord in arms.

Though sways the balance of the strife,
  From losses near, to gains afar,
Her Faith shines steadfast on his head,
  As on the ship the Polar Star.

Let brother question brother's might,
  And man's distrust of man be rife,
'T is not in Woman's heart to doubt
  The pow'r that won and rules the wife.

Through all the battle's storm of sounds,
  The crash of death, the host's rejoice,
In that, she hears his sabre-stroke,
  In this, his own triumphant voice.

And if for grace the foeman bend,
  Though ev'ry lip with fury foam,

His hand falls softly through her pray'r,
  As on his Darling's head at home.

So, should the land refuse to praise,
  An ocean shall his glory be, —
A Hope as tireless as the wave,
  A love as boundless as the sea.

THE MAN OF FEELING.

ALAS! for him whose simple soul,
  A garden cherish'd by the sun,
Lies open to the public way,
  For ev'ry foot to tread upon.

And whether in a wanton mood,
  Or by a selfish purpose led,
Each passer tramples on the verge
  Where all his tend'rest feelings spread.

And then his wounded nature feels —
  What his alone can understand,
The flow'r that 's broken by the heel,
  Can ne'er be mended by the hand.

From gentle instinct taught to love
  The meanest creature of his race,
He took his image of the World
  When God was shining in his face;

Nor dream'd that earth could wear a Cross,
  Save, as it fell, while glory blazed,
The noonday Shadow of a Christ,
  With arms in Benediction raised.

And not 'till bleeding from the world,
  He learns the heartless world it is ;
That ruder souls the gentler crush,
  And all are rude to such as his.

Though turning to his fellow-men,
  With hope in each a friend to meet,
He stands as lonely as a tree
  Upon a city's stony street;

For, ever to the open hand,
  The perfect trust, the guileless air,
Not even Charity is kind,
  And Manhood doubts a Man is there.

Then, shrinking stricken to himself,
  With silent grieving desolate,
He lives a coward to the wind,
  And fears the things he cannot hate.

There is a sinking of his soul,
  A sudden shock of age and care ;
As one who in a mirror sees
  The first gray streaking of his hair.

And growing tremulous with dread
  Of what one word, one look, may be,
He dares not seek to make a friend,
  Lest love should die of jealousy.

Thus, friendless and alone he goes,
  To none a prize, to all a prey ;

Like water dripping on a rock,
  By trifles wears his life away.

And yet there is an inward light
  To keep his soul from growing dark,
Through which his nature's incense breaks,
  Like music breaking from the lark;

For, though the world sweeps coldly by,
  Or pauses but to cast a dart,
There 's something cannot chill nor die, —
  His grand simplicity of heart.

JOHN BROWN.

GOD holds His scales in a poise between
The deed Unjust and the end Unseen,
And the sparrow's fall in the one is weigh'd
By the Lord's own Hand in the other laid.

Where leads the path to our Sunset gate,
And flow'rs the heart of a new-born State,
Are the hopes of an old man's waning years,
'Neath the headstones worn by an old man's tears.

When sinks the sun in the prairie West,
His last red ray is the headstone's crest;
And the mounds he laves in a crimson flood
Are a Soldier's pay in the coin of blood!

Do ye ask who rear'd those headstones there,
And plaited thorns for a sire's gray hair?
And by whom was the Land's great debt thus paid
To the Soldier old, in the graves they made?

Shrink, Pity! shrink, at the question dire;
And, Honor, burn in a blush of fire!
Turn, God of the Just, from the page thine eyes,
Or the Sin, till the Judgment, never dies!

They shared the Land he had fought to save,
From a foreign foe that cross'd the wave,
When he struck for the Weak against the Strong
And march'd to a strife as his whole life long.

They came of the clime whose soft warm breath
Is earth's fair youth, and a life in death;
Where the Summer chains but a Spring to Spring,
And the songs of birds through the whole year ring;

Where falling leaves are the cups that grew
To catch the spray of the new leaf's dew,
And the winds through the blossom'd depths that creep
Are the sighs of Time in a noonday sleep.

But lurk'd a taint in the clime so blest,
Like serpent coil'd in a ring-dove's nest,
And the hateful sight to the eye it gave,
Was the brand of chains on a low-brow'd Slave!

The Soldier old, at his sentry-post,
Where the sun's last trail of light is lost,
Was shamed with the shame of the Land he loved,
And the old, old pride in his bosom moved.

He cried to the land, Beware, Beware
The symbol'd Curse in the Bondman there!
And a prophet's soul in the hour came down
To be heard in the voice of old John Brown.

He cried: and the ingrate answer came
In words of lead from a tongue of flame;

And dyed was his hearth in the blood of kin,
Where his dear ones fell for the Nation's Sin!

O matchless deed! that a fiend might scorn;
O deed of shame! for a world to mourn;
'T was a Soldier's pay in his blood most dear,
And a land to mock at a Father's tear!

Is 't strange that the tranquil soul of age
Was turn'd to strife in a madman's rage?
Is it strange that the cry of blood did seem
Like the call of drums in a soldier's dream?

Is 't strange the clank of the Bondman's chain
Should drive the Wrong to the old man's brain,
To flame in his heart to a santon's zeal,
And his weak arm mate to the vengeful steel?

The bane of Wrong to its depth had gone,
The sword of Right from its sheath was drawn;
But the Slave in the swamp heard not his cry,
And the old man had arm'd him but to die.

Go call him Mad, that he did not quail
When broke his blade on the unblest mail:
Ye may call him mad, that he struck alone,
That he made of the land's dark Curse his own;

But the Eye of God look'd down and saw
A just life lost by an unjust law;
And black was the day with the Lord's own frown
When the Southern Cross was a martyr's Crown!

Apostate clime! from the blood then shed
Was a cry for vengeance on your head,
That should weigh you down 'neath the falling rod
When your red right hand should be stretch'd to God.

Behold the price of the life you took:
At its last great gasp a whole world shook;
And the despot deed that could one heart break,
From their slavish sleep made a million wake!

Not all alone did the victim fall
By the deed that brought him to your thrall;
In the old man's wrong was a Nation's part,
And you struck your blow at a Nation's heart!

When the freemen-host was at your door,
A Voice went forth with a stern "No more!"
To the Curse of the Land, whose swift redeem
Was the thought that had vision'd John Brown's dream.

To the Country's Wrong, the Country's stain,
It proved as the scythe to yielding grain;
And the pow'r of the strong to spread it forth
Was the arm and the soul of the chainless North.

From the East and West and North they came,
In sweeping might of a prairie flame,
With a viewless form for their unknown guide,—
A form that was born when the Old Man died!

The Soldier old in his grave may rest
Beside his dead in the free-born West;

But a red ray falls on the headstones there,
Like the Lord's reply to a martyr's pray'r.

He may sleep in peace 'neath greenwood pall,
For the land's great heart hath heard his call;
And a people's Will and a people's Might,
In his name they have slain the Wrong for Right.

He nobly dies for his own dear Land
Who falls by the foreign foeman's brand;
But a nobler rank'd with her martyrs he
When 't is o'er Herself is her Victory.

The Honor saved unto those who live
Is gauge of the Honor death can give
To the life laid down in the hangman's cords,
Or the life blown out in a wind of swords.

Not all in vain is the lesson taught —
A great soul's Dream is the world's New Thought;
And the Scaffold mark'd with a death sublime
Is the Throne ordain'd for the coming time!

THE FALLS.

I.

DROPS of water, —
Limpid water!
Sparkling, darkling, steeping, creeping,
Through the grassy lattice peeping,
Like the royal elfin's eyes,
When on sever'd leaf he lies;
Trickling on in blending balls,
Flowing,
Going,
With a murmur, to the Falls.

II.

Rills of water, —
Childish water!
Shiv'ring, quiv'ring, straying, playing,
Where the sober stones are staying;
Rocking lilies up and down,
Bearing many a foamy crown,
Through the lonely woodland halls;
Sliding,
Gliding,
Far away to join the Falls.

III.

Sheets of water, —
Laughing water!
Hissing, kissing, wrinkling, twinkling,
With a clear, melodious tinkling,
Deep reflecting banner clouds,
Furl'd above, like vessel shrouds
When the shadow on them crawls;
Tossing,
Crossing,
To the music of the Falls.

IV.

Folds of water, —
Crystal water!
Dashing, splashing, whirling, curling,
Mistral standard wide unfurling,
In a charge adown the hill.
Where the rocks are lying still,
In their moss-incrusted stalls,
Jutting,
Cutting
Liquid ribbons for the Falls.

V.

Streams of water, —
Rushing water!
Roaring, pouring, gleaming, streaming,
Like a mighty river dreaming
Of a tempest on the sea,
Sweeping down in midnight glee

From the crested ocean walls;
　　　　Boiling,
　　　　Toiling,
To the volume of the Falls.

VI.

　　　　Floods of water, —
　　　　Surging water!
Moaning, groaning, wailing, railing,
While the ancient tree is failing,
Like a straying soldier lost,
Bending to an armèd host;
Sounding martial bugle-calls,
　　　　Gushing,
　　　　Rushing
To the battle of the Falls.

VII.

　　　　Hosts of water, —
　　　　Madden'd water!
Rumbling, tumbling, sweeping, leaping,
Carnival of rivers keeping,
Breaking, with resistless might,
From the cloud-surrounded height,
Form'd in sinking crystal walls;
　　　　Wreathing,
　　　　Seething,
With the thunder of the Falls.

VIII.

　　　　Veils of water, —
　　　　Tinted water!

Weaving, cleaving, vining, twining,
All a magic arch designing,
Painted with the glowing dyes,
Of Italia's ev'ning skies,
And of Fairies' em'rald palls ;
            Blending,
            Bending,
In a bow across the Falls.

LEONORE.

I SAW her in the bright saloon,
  As I had seen before
The proudest women of the land,
  But none like Leonore ;
So wrapt in living poetry
  Was ev'ry grace she wore.

The pure camellias in her hair
  Were not so fair as she ;
And in the roses of her cheeks
  My eager eyes could see
The banners of a regal pride,
  That said : Come, worship me !

The jewels on her brow of snow,
  Beneath the chandeliers,
Seem'd like the record of a life
  Inscribed in frozen tears
Upon a marble temple's front,
  With gold to link the years.

I heard the rustling of a robe,
  Like leaves before the rain,

And throngs roll'd back on either side,
  Like waves upon the main
When some mermaiden walks at night,
  With Tritons in her train.

And then a light, familiar step
  Prophetic fancy heard,
As gentle in its airy fall
  As that of woodland bird;
Yet ev'ry tap upon the floor
  Was an unspoken word!

I saw a smile divide the lips
  That oft had honor'd mine;
But there was something in the smile
  My heart could not define;
So superficial was its beam,
  And yet so near divine.

She spoke, but in an alter'd tone
  From that I once had known
When she, in other robes than these,
  Had smiled on me alone,
And whisper'd, O, so tenderly!
  That she was all my own.

We parted, e'en as strangers part
  Upon a foreign shore,
When each is to the other dead,
  As they had been before
The paths of their existence met,
  To meet again no more.

I saw her once again that night,
  When one was called to sing
A ballad of the olden time,
  Of wooing and a ring,
And of a bride unsullied turn'd
  Into a guilty thing.

O Leonore! my ling'ring hope
  Was blighted with the tear
That wash'd thy fatal pride away,
  And roll'd, as thou didst hear
A father's hopeless sorrows borne
  In music to thine ear.

And all my love was banish'd then,
  But pity took its place;
For in the silent agony
  Reflected in thy face
I saw, beneath the badge of shame,
  An old, familiar grace.

THE MIRROR.

"Inspicere tanquam in speculum, in vitas omnium jubeo."

SPEAK! thou pale and staring Phantom,
From the picture in the glass;
Now is the prophetic moment,
Tell me what shall come to pass!

Thou art looking to the future
With those sunken eyes of thine,
And the fire reflected in them
Kindles on a distant shrine.

From the valley of the Present,
Rank with unavailing tears,
Is there not an upward passage,
Paved with future years on years?

Leading upward o'er the mountain
In whose shade I wander now?
Leading upward, leading onward
To the Temple on its brow?

Tell me, silent seer, I pray thee,
Is there not a pow'r sublime,
That can make a yearning mortal
Rise superior to his time?

Must the spectres of our sorrows,
  Real in the bitter Past,
Keep so near us in the present
  That their chill is forward cast?

Can the mem'ry of a harsher
  Note upon the spirit's strings
Drown the music of the Heaven
  Deathless aspiration brings?

Can a chain of cold denials,
  Growing greater as they pass,
Fetter down a soul forever?
  Speak! thou Phantom of the glass.

Must the naked soul be measured
  By a standard rear'd of pelf?
Ope those mocking lips and tell me,
  O my torturing Second Self!

Thou art silent as the marble
  Bearing many a sculptured name,
Once of those who ask'd the question,
  Dying ere their answers came;

But a shadow thin, uncertain,
  All thy features plays about,
And within thine eyes reflected
  Is the torture of a Doubt!

Get thee gone, thou evil prophet!
  Mine shall be a nobler lot

Than thy coward look would make it;
  Get thee gone, and mock me not!

Vain the words. That mocking Phantom
  Evermore will linger there,
Chilling all my mortal being
  With its cold and Doubting stare;

Ever near me, right before me
  While I pause and when I pass;
And, howe'er I strive to shun it,
  All the world is still its glass.

THE BOATSWAIN'S CALL.

THE lights upon the river's brink
  In constellation bright,
Are winking down upon the tide
  That twinkles through the night,
When in a gayly dancing skiff
  The boatswain leaves his ship,
And as his oars a moment cease
  Within the flood to dip,
        He winds his call,
        The boatswain's cheery call.

A maiden stands upon the shore,
  Where land and ocean meet,
And breakers cast their pearly gifts
  In homage at her feet;
While through the causeway of the night
  She gazes o'er the sea,
To where a stately frigate rides
  In lonely majesty,
        And waits the call,
        The gallant boatswain's call.

"O, tarry not, my boatswain bold,"
  Her parted lips would say;

But when the heart is vex'd with doubt,
  The soul can only pray;
And sorely doubtful is the maid,
  Till on her ear there falls
The music of the merriest,
  The clearest, best of calls, —
          A winding call,
          Her faithful boatswain's call.

A shining keel is on the sand,
  The oars are laid aside,
And to the shore the sailor leaps
  To greet his chosen bride;
His arms about her waist are thrown,
  And through her rosy lips
He breathes a dainty boatswain's call,
  Though not the call of ships;
          But Cupid's call,
          The boatswain Cupid's call.

And when the moon has drawn a path
  Of light upon the sea,
A skiff is floating o'er the deep,
  To where a frigate free
Is nestled in the ocean's breast,
  With all her canvas furl'd;
Though ere the morn makes Hesper fade
  Upon a waking world,
          "Make sail, men, all!"
          Will round the boatswain's call.

A shadow follows in her wake,
  And through its depths is seen
The figure of a widow'd wife
  Upon the shore of green;
And ever as the tempest moans
  Above the mocking wave,
A sound is wafted to her ears
  From out a moving grave, —
        A boatswain's call,
        A ghostly boatswain's call.

THE MIDNIGHT WATCH.

SOLDIER, soldier, wan and gray,
  Standing there so very still,
On the outpost looking South,
  What is there to-night to kill?

Through the mist, that rises thick
  From the noisome marsh around,
I can see thee like a shade
  Cast from something underground.

And I know that thou art old,
  For thy features, sharp and thin,
Cut their lines upon the shroud
  Damply folding thee within.

Fit art thou to watch and guard
  O'er the brake and o'er the bog;
By the glitter of thine eyes
  Thou canst pierce a thicker fog.

Tell me, soldier grim and old,
  If thy tongue is free to say,
What thou seest, looking South
  In that still and staring way?

Yonderward the fires may glow
  Of a score of rebel camps ;
But thou canst not see their lights,
  Through the chilling dews and damps.

Silent still, and motionless ?
  Get thee to the tents behind,
Where the flag for which we fight
  Plays a foot-ball to the wind.

Get thee to the bankments high,
  Where a thousand cannon sleep,
While the call that bids them wake
  Bids a score of millions weep.

Thou shalt find an army there,
  Working out the statesman's plots,
While a poison banes the land,
  And a noble nation rots.

Thou shalt find a soldier-host
  Tied and rooted to its place,
Like a woman cow'd and dumb,
  Staring Treason in the face.

Dost thou hear me ? Speak, or move !
  And if thou would'st pass the line,
Give the password of the night, —
  Halt ! and give the countersign.

God of Heaven ! what is this
  Sounding through the frosty air,

In a cadence stern and slow,
From the figure looming there?

"Sentry, thou hast spoken well," —
Through the mist the answer came, —
"I am wrinkled, grim, and old,
May'st thou live to be the same!

"Thou art here to keep a watch
Over prowlers coming nigh;
I can show thee, looking South,
What is hidden from thine eye.

"Here, the loyal armies sleep;
There, the foe awaits them all;
Who can tell before the time
Which shall triumph, which shall fall?

"O, but war 's a royal game,
Here a move and there a pause;
Little recks the dazzled world
What may be the winner's cause.

"In the roar of sweating guns,
In the crash of sabres cross'd,
Wisdom dwindles to a fife,
Justice in the smoke is lost.

"But there is a mightier blow
Than the rain of lead and steel,
Falling from a heavier hand
Than the one the vanquish'd feel.

"Let the armies of the North
Rest them thus for longer night;
Not with them the issue lies
'Twixt the pow'rs of Wrong and Right.

"Through the fog that wraps us round
I can see as with a glass,
Far beyond the rebel hosts,
Fires that cluster, pause, and pass.

"From the wayside and the wood,
From the cabin and the swamp,
Crawl the harbingers of blood,
Black as night, with torch and lamp.

"Now they blend in one dense throng;
Hark! they whisper, as in ire, —
Catch the word before it dies, —
Hear the horrid murmur, — 'Fire!'

"Mothers, with your babes at rest,
Maidens in your dreaming-land, —
Brothers, children, — wake ye all!
The Avenger is at hand.

"Born by thousands in a flash,
Angry flames bescourge the air,
And the howlings of the blacks
Fan them to a fiercer glare.

"Crash the windows, burst the doors,
Let the helpless call for aid;

From the hell within they rush
   On the negro's reeking blade.

" Through the flaming doorway arch,
   Half-dress'd women frantic dart;
Demon ! spare that kneeling girl —
   God ! the knife is in her heart.

" By his hair so thin and gray
   Forth they drag the aged sire ;
First, a stab to stop his pray'r, —
   Hurl him back into the fire.

" What ! a child, a mother's pride,
   Crying shrilly with affright !
Dash the axe upon her skull,
   Show no mercy, — she is White.

" Louder, louder roars the flame,
   Blotting out the Southern home ;
Fainter grow the dying shrieks,
   Fiercer cries of vengeance come.

" Turn, ye armies, where ye stand,
   Glaring in each other's eyes ;
While ye halt, a cause is won ;
   While ye wait, a despot dies.

' Greater vict'ry has been gain'd
   Than the longest sword secures,
And the Wrong has been wash'd out
   With a purer blood than yours."

Soldier, by my mother's pray'r!
  Thou dost act a demon's part;
Tell me, ere I strike thee dead,
  Whence thou comest, who thou art?

Back! I will not let thee pass, —
  Silent still thou comest on! —
Soldier, soldier, where art thou?
  Vanish'd, — like a shadow gone!

THE ROMANCE OF THE OLD.

THOUGH bends the hoary head with years
  In reverential grace,
As bowing meekly unto God
  When nearest to His face ;
Yet lives there something of the child,
  One spark amid the cold,
To brighten with a gleam of youth
  The Romance of the Old.

Not all the throng of worldly cares
  That sadden life's decline,
Can leave the human heart without
  Some one Ideal's shrine ;
For if Realities have proved
  What childhood ne'er foretold,
Still clings the fiction's charm about
  The Romance of the Old.

O lover, in thy blushing pride,
  O sweetheart, in thy walks,
Turn not in angry haste away
  Because an old man talks ;

But think the twinkle of his eye,
O'er jokes so often doled,
Reflects thine own romance within
The Romance of the Old.

The hand that hangs the Christmas Tree
With quaint, ingenious toys,
May lack the whiteness of the girl's,
The quickness of the boy's;
Yet in the loving heart that bids
Such fruit the leaves infold,
Are children's dreams, renew'd, to guide
The Romance of the Old.

I saw returning from a church
A fond and happy pair;
And He with look and step elate,
And She with modest air:
Behind them came two stooping forms
As happy; — but, behold!
They wept; for weeping marketh oft
The Romance of the Old!

To manhood in its hardy prime
And womanhood the young,
'T is given perfect joy to show
By music from the tongue;
But tears refine the wither'd cheek
Where many a tear hath roll'd,
When tenderness through pleasure thrills
The Romance of the Old.

All blessings on the sacred head
  That wears the silver crown,
And blessings on the shaking hand
  That smoothes its brightness down ;
And blessings on the shrunken lips,
  To kindness, only, bold,
Whose very benedictions breathe
  The Romance of the Old !

And whether at the hearth of Home,
  Or in the world around,
Let's thank the Father of us all
  For mercy so profound ;
That, as in Age begins the sleep
  When heart and hand are cold,
Still glows a dream of Youth within
  The Romance of the Old.

MIDSUMMER.

MOODILY a hazy glory,
  Falling from a dome of light,
Held in quiet spell around me,
  Veils my sight.

Sleepily the rose and lily
  Nod along the garden wall;
Little care they for the future,
  If at all.

Listlessly the dainty zephyr
  Ripples down the yellow field,
Fitfully exposing daisies
  Half conceal'd.

Heavily the wood keeps swaying,
  Giving many a sleepy start,
While a little bird talks music
  To its heart.

Languidly the shining river
  Curls its silver in the sun,
While its thousand water-dimples
  Blend in one.

Weaily the ox is dozing,
  Right amid the bearded wheat,
Winking at the bluebird tripping
  Round his feet.

Cosily old Dobbin feedeth
  In the shadow of the oak,
With the easy halter lying
  Where it broke.

Drowsily above the meadow
  Hums the vagrant, careless fly;
Can it be he is as lazy
  Half as I?

Dreamily I watch the Summer
  Planting sunlight where she will;
May her beaming presence leave me
  Dreaming still!

ENGLAND TO AMERICA.

(1861.)

WESTWARD, westward flies the eagle, westward
with the setting sun,
To an eyrie growing golden in the morning just begun ;
Where the world is new in promise of a virgin nation's
love,
And the grand results of ages germs of nobler ages
prove ;

Where a prophecy of greatness runs through all the
soul of youth,
And the miracle of Freedom blesses in a living truth ;
Where the centuries unnumber'd narrow to a single
night,
And their trophies are but planets wheeling round a
later light.

Where the headlands breast the Ocean sweeping round
creation's East,
And the prairies roll in blossoms to the Ocean of the
West ;
Where the voices of the seas are blended o'er a nation's
birth,
In the harmony of Nature's hymn to Liberty on earth.

Land of Promise ! Revelation of a royalty that springs
From a grander depth of purple than the heritage of kings, —
From the inner purple cherish'd at the thrones of lives sublime,
Cast in glorious consecration 'neath the plough of Father Time, —

Home of Freedom, hope of millions born and slain and yet to be,
Shall the spirit of the bondless, caught from heaven, fail in thee?
Shall the watching world behold thee falling from thy starry height?
Like a meteor, in thine ending leaving only darker night!

O my kinsmen, O my brothers, — fellow-heirs of Saxon hearts,
Lo, the Eagle quits his eyrie swifter than a swallow darts,
And the lurid flame of battle burns within his angry eye,
Glowing like a living ember cast in vengeance from the sky.

At thy hearth a foe has risen, fiercer yet to burn and kill,
That he was thy chosen brother, — friend no more, but brother still;
For the bitter tide of hatred deeper runs and fiercer grows,
As the pleading voice of Nature addeth self-reproach to blows.

Strike! and in the ghastly horrors of a fratricidal war
Learn the folly of thy wanderings from the guiding Northern Star;
What were all thy gains and glories, to creation's fatal loss
In thy Freedom's crucifixion on the cruel Southern Cross?

O my brothers narrow-sighted, — O my brothers slow to hear
What the phantoms of the fallen ever whisper in the ear;
God is just, and from the ruins of the temple rent in twain
Rises up the invocation of a warning breathed in vain.

All thy pillars reel around thee from the fury of the blow,
And the fires upon thine altars fade and flicker to and fro;
Call the vigor of thy manhood into arms from head to foot,
Strike! and in thy strife with error let the blow be at the root.

So thy war shall wear the glory of a purpose to refine
From the dross of early folly all the honor that is thine;
So thine arms shall gather friendship to the standard of a cause,
Blending in its grand approval British hearts and British laws.

Form thy heroes into armies from the mart and from
the field,
And their ranks shall stretch around thee in a bristling,
living shield;
Take the loyal beggar's offer; for the war whose
cause is just
Breathes the soul of noblest daring into forms of meanest dust.

Let thy daughters wreathe their chaplets for the fore-
heads of the brave,
Let thy daughters wed the lovers marching from them
to the grave;
Woman's love is built the strongest when it rests on
woman's pride,
Better be a soldier's widow than a meek civilian's bride.

Onward let thine Eagles lead thee, where the livid
Southern sun
Courts the incense for the heavens of a righteous battle
won;
And the bright Potomac, winding through the fields
unto the sea,
Shall no longer mark the libel — what is bond and
what is free.

Rising from the fierce ordeal, wash'd in blood and
purified,
See the future stretch before thee, limitless on ev'ry
side;
And in all the deep'ning envy of the nations wed to sloth,
Read the record of thy progress, see the mirror of thy
growth.

Rising from thy purifying, like a giant from his rest,
Thou shalt find thy praise an echo from the East unto the West;
Thou shalt find thy love a message from the South unto the North,
Each its past mistake of duty finding out and casting forth.

And thy States in new communion, by the blood they all have shed,
Shall be wedded to each other in the pardon of the dead;
Each, a scale of steel to cover vital part from foreign wrong,
All, a coat of armor guarding that to which they All belong.

Thou shalt measure seas with navies, span the earth with iron rails,
Catch the dawn upon thy banner and the sunset on thy sails;
Northern halls of ice shall echo to thy sailor's merry note,
And the standard of thy soldier o'er the Southern isle shall float.

Turning to thy mother, England, thou shalt find her making boast
Of the Great Republic westward, born of strength that she has lost;
And thy Saxon blood shall join ye, never to be torn apart,
Moving onward to the future, hand in hand and heart to heart.

THE DEATH OF THE ROSES.

WHO shall tell the roses now
  Where their missing loves are lying,
Buried under softest snows,
  By the sweetest torture dying, —
Dying, like the morning's ray
Lapt and lost in perfect day?

Dainty Zephyr, cherish'd oft
  By the flow'rs to their undoing,
Have you found the Roses' grave
  Here, or there, in all your wooing, —
Wooing wide and wooing free,
Constant to Inconstancy?

Brief the tale the Zephyr tells,
  How the pair he half discover'd
Lurking 'neath a virgin's veil,
  As about the place he hover'd, —
Hover'd, till in orange sprays
Quick he lost them from his gaze.

Orange Blossoms, frail as fair,
  Loved of all who wear the kirtle,

Know ye if the Roses lost
  Kiss'd the Cypress, or the Myrtle?
Myrtle, ask the Cypress, thou,
Where the Roses died, and how?

This the tale the blossoms tell,
  Whisp'ring one unto the other,
Softly, softly breathing low
  As they would the secret smother, —
Smother from the Blue-bell's ear,
Bent in expectation near.

On the cheeks the lover wed
  Grew the Roses; there they perish'd
When, before the altar, Love
  Rivals to the Roses cherish'd, —
Cherish'd Lilies for the Bride, —
Then and there the Roses died!

THE FALLEN LEAF.

'TWAS green a little while ago,
  And moist with all the Summer's breath;
But now it flutters to and fro,
  And, touch'd with Autumn, bleeds to death.

First when it hung upon the bough,
  The earliest leaflet of the tree,
The branch that claim'd it made a vow
  To cherish it with constancy.

But as its sister-leaves appear'd,
  And each her newer charms display'd,
It ceased, alas! to be endear'd,
  And droop'd neglected in the shade.

Ah me! how many a human thing,
  From loving first and best of all,
Has blossom'd earliest in the Spring,
  To wither soonest in the Fall!

NO MORE.

HUSH'D be the song and the love-notes of gladness
That broke with the morn from the cottager's door —
Muffle the tread in the soft stealth of sadness,
For one who returneth, whose chamber-lamp burneth
No more.

Silent he lies on the broad path of glory,
Where withers ungarner'd the red crop of war.
Grand is his couch, though the pillows are gory,
'Mid forms that shall battle, 'mid guns that shall rattle
No more.

Soldier of Freedom, thy marches are ended, —
The dreams that were prophets of triumph are o'er ;
Death with the night of thy manhood is blended, —
The bugle shall call thee, the fight shall enthrall thee
No more.

Far to the Northward the banners are dimming,
And faint comes the tap of the drummers before ;
Low in the tree-tops the swallow is skimming ;
Thy comrades shall cheer thee, the weakest shall fear thee
No more.

Far to the Westward the day is at vespers,
And bows down its head, like a priest, to adore,
Soldier, the twilight for thee has no whispers,
The night shall forsake thee, the morn shall awake thee
No more.

Wide o'er the plain, where the white tents are gleaming,
In spectral array, like the graves they 're before —
One there is empty, where once thou wert dreaming
Of deeds that are boasted, of One that is toasted
No more.

When the Commander to-morrow proclaimeth
A list of the brave for the nation to store,
Thou shalt be known with the heroes he nameth,
Who wake from their slumbers, who answer their numbers
No more.

Hush'd be the song and the love-notes of gladness
That broke with the morn from the cottager's door,—
Muffle the tread in the soft stealth of sadness,
For one who returneth, whose chamber-lamp burneth
No more.

THE HOPES OF DAYS GONE BY.

YE royal years, whose crowns on crosses rest,
Rich in all honors, deathless in all fame ;
Grand with the echoes of a god's reply
To the wild pray'r Ambition gives the breast, —
Where is the Promise, nobler far, that bless'd
The Hopes of Days gone by ?

Shadows of shades, that chill and mock the soul !
Spectres to Mem'ry of the Unfulfill'd ;
Harsh with unkind reproaches to the eye
That looks on all, and misses yet the whole —
O flow'rs of youth, that all your sweetness stole ! —
The Hopes of Days gone by.

Fond, foolish dreams ! of childish fever born ;
Vain as the airy cities of the clouds
By poet-fancy traced against the sky ;
Frail as the bubble on the new wave worn,
Yet pure and holy as the hush of morn, —
The Hopes of Days gone by !

Years, weary years, with all the woes ye win
For throned Misfortune, there 's a moment still
In anguish richer than to know and die, —
When Boyhood ends, and Manhood's cares begin,
To feel and know that naught was real in
The Hopes of Days gone by !

WINTER.

THE Northern winds, like sorrow stirr'd to wrath,
Moan through the vista of the planet's path,
And in the world's chill ev'ning just begun
Fan to a hueless fire a dying sun.

Upon the sea, where water-mountains rise
And hurl the spray in brilliants to the skies,
A breath of Odin, from a frosty lip,
Show'rs back dead lilies round about the ship.

Then, as the billows sweeping to the Pole
Dimly through Arctic sunset flushes roll,
Slow from the deep a crystal city grows,
Wall'd with rock mirrors, roof'd with royal snows.

Sandal'd with ice, and veil'd in silver mist,
Touch'd by the day to tints of amethyst,
The bride of Charon gains the silent shore,
Queen of the Year that rules the world no more.

Dead to the passions, stricken Nature sleeps,
Like a dead mother when her infant weeps;
Dead to the morning light, the ev'ning hours;
Dead! for her soul hath vanish'd with the flow'rs.

Lone in his many-column'd forest hall
Paces the wolf, with hungry eye for all ;
High on the leafless branch the starving crow
Droops, like an omen of a doom below.

Far stretch the fields in ruin desolate,
Blank as the parchment of unwritten Fate,
Gray with the ashes of a harvest done,
Sad with the mem'ry of a reaper gone.

Sharp through the day's eclipse the road curls round,
Linking the doorway with the churchyard ground ;
Showing in all its length one shape alone, —
A crouching beggar, frozen to the bone !

With but that beggar's eye to mark his fall,
And he a-dying — dead and dying all !
The Old Year bows his head upon his breast,
While his last sun goes down to endless rest.

Then gath'ring to his royal brow a cloud,
Fraught with a crown of ice and ermine shroud,
Ere yet the New Year's bells begin to ring,
Together die the Beggar and the King.

THE ANCIENT CAPTAIN.

THE smiles of an ev'ning were shed on the sea,
And its wave-lips laugh'd through their beard-
ings of foam;
And the eyes of an ev'ning were mirror'd beneath
Both the shroud of the ship and her home.

As Time knows an end, so that sea knew a shore,
Afar in a beautiful, tropical clime,
Where Love with the Life of each being is blent,
In soft, psychological Rhyme.

O, grand was the shore, when deserted and still
It breasted the silver-mail'd hosts of the Deep,
And like the last bulwark of Nature it seem'd,
'Twixt Death and an Innocent's sleep.

But grander it was to the eyes of a knight,
When, clad in his armor, he stood on the sands,
And held to his bosom its essence of Life, —
An heiress of titles and lands.

Ah, fondly he gazed on the face of the maid!
And blush-spoken fondness replied to his look;
While heart answer'd heart with a feverish beat,
And hand press'd the hand that it took.

"Fair lady of mine," said the knight, stooping low,
"Before I depart for the banquet of Death,
I crave a new draught from the fountain of Life,
Whose waters are all in thy breath.

"The breast that is fill'd with thine image alone
May safely defy the dread tempest of steel;
For while all its thoughts are of love and of thee,
What peril of Self can it feel?"

He paused; and the silence that follow'd his words
Was spread like a Hope, 'twixt a Dream and a truth;
And in it his fancy created a world
Wrought out of the dreams of his youth.

Then shadows crept over the beautiful face
Turn'd up to the sky in the pale streaming light,
As shadows sweep over the orient pearl,
Far down in the river at night.

"You 're going," she said, "where the fleets are in leash,
Where plumed is a knight for each wave of the sea,
Yet all the wide Ocean shall have but One wave,
One ship and One sailor for me!"

He left her, as leaveth the god of a dream
The portals that close with a heavier sleep;
And then, as he sprang to the shallop in wait,
The rowers push'd off in the Deep.

CHRISTMAS EVE.

I.

THE solemn winds were sighing for the echoes, dead and dying,
That were wont to teach them music when their lutes were on the trees;
And the snow in tides was curling, dancing here and there, and whirling
Fitful ashes of the lilies on the waves of ghostly seas.

II.

Like haunted mausoleum, 'neath the spell of a Te Deum,
That should lay the restless spirit of some disembodied woe,
Stretch'd the world in awful slumber, while the ocean pulsed the number
Of its years, upon that Christmas Eve within the Long Ago.

III.

The trees, all wan, and tatter'd, spread their wither'd arms, and shatter'd,
To receive their shrouds of ermine as they fell in fringes down;

And each tall and spectral steeple, keeping guard o'er
hidden people,
Caught the heav'nly benefaction in a mitre or a
crown.

IV.

The awe-struck soul of Nature, turning softly from the
Future,
Look'd, in dreams, through weary ages back to a
celestial morn ;
And while snows were sadly falling, and the wind to
wind was calling,
Felt the glory of that moment when Our Blessed
Lord was born !

V.

Afar the wings were shaken, that the winter's gnomes
had taken,
And they shaped and cast their feather'd flakes on
palace and on cot ;
But though all the rest had slumber'd that the living
world had number'd,
Still one there was who cowering felt, although he
heard them not.

VI.

Where crazy casements rattled, and a door uneven
battled
With the grim and ice-mail'd spearsmen charging
blindly on the blast,
Dwelt the Watcher, old and lonely, with a bitter
mem'ry only
To keep him present company and to link him with
the past.

VII.

His garments, thin and tatter'd, o'er his poor old form
were scatter'd,
Like the shrivell'd leaves of autumn o'er a fallen
forest tree ;
And his hoary locks, that blended with a silv'ry beard
untended,
Framed features pinch'd with years of want and
piteous poverty.

VIII.

No fagot blazed to cheer him, and the empty cup-
board near him
Was eloquent of all that lowliest poverty can bear,
While there burn'd a single taper, whose each faint
and sickly caper
Show'd hideous spiders, webb'd and toss'd upon the
frosty air.

IX.

But spite of all the squalor, and the misery and dolor,
Which relentlessly had bound him in the most forlorn estate,
There around him clung a glory, like to some unwritten
story
That, revealing from a ruin, tells the temple once
was great.

X.

Within the taper's glimmer, and while yet it faded
dimmer,
Like a vague and taunting spectre of the world's
misguided dress,

He sat with all the seeming e'en of one in memory dreaming,
And clasp'd in his poor, quivering hands a little Golden Cross.

XI.

Before the days of trouble, 't was a woman wore the bauble —
A maiden true and holy as the spirit of a prayer;
Angel wings in all her motions, and the souls of living oceans
Prison'd in the eyes reflecting all the sunlight of her hair.

XII.

A Father's Faith was round her, and in sunny chains it bound her
To her young heart's best ideal of a Mother gone Above;
But, alas! the chains were broken, when the words in secret spoken
Tore her soul from out its heaven with a troubled dream of Love.

XIII.

Then came a waking morrow, when the depths of tearless sorrow
Render'd up their dead in curses that would stir a god to fear;
And while Christmas bells were ringing, and the Christmas choirs were singing,
All the old man's Hope went down to death as waned the dying year.

XIV.

Upon the highway wending, soon a figure, slight and bending,
Swept by the happier beggar, who in pity ceased to grieve ;
For the Curse had bred a terror in that stricken child of Error,
And she fled, she knew not whither, on that darksome Christmas Eve.

XV.

The old man, grim and lonely, waited — waited for this only —
A moment — e'en a second — in the short'ning of his days,
To make the Curse a Blessing — for his sorrowing soul confessing,
Left his loss a double torture, with the Lost before his gaze.

XVI.

But years roll'd on unheeding, — deaf to all his hopes and pleading
That some gentle day would bring her, like God's pardon, to his door ;
And the Curse, in vengeance utter'd, ever round his being mutter'd
From the likeness of a Shadow — Her last shadow on the floor !

XVII.

He sat, that Christmas Even, thus the bann'd of Earth
and Heaven,
With the best and only token of the angel that had
been ;
And the glittering Cross, uplifted, seem'd by God's
approval gifted
With pow'r to weigh a father's tears against a
father's sin.

XVIII.

While yet he gazed in sadness, rose the winds in sudden madness
And dash'd down the door between them and the
hoary watcher there,
And upon the threshold kneeling, with no gloom of
night concealing,
He beheld Her, as he knew her, with the sunlight
in her hair !

XIX.

" At last ! " The sentence spoken from a heart long
lone and broken
Told of all the weary sorrows that a life had made
its store.
The kneeling Spirit listen'd, and the Cross all glorious
glisten'd ;
And behold the haunting Shadow faded from the
dimming floor !

XX.

"My sin is all forgiven! and you pray for me in Heaven!"
The old man wildly whisper'd with his faltering lips apart;
The Spirit grasps his fingers, for a moment pitying lingers,
Then enfolds the Sacred Symbol with his hands unto Her heart!

XXI.

Like music born of Sorrow, but as sweet as Love's to-morrow,
There were heard these words of comfort, and all lovingly they fell:
"I am worthy now to wear it. Father — Mother — you can spare it;
For your Child, through deep repentance, made the Curse a Holy Spell."

XXII.

The old man's voice resounded, and from wall and beam rebounded,
With grandeur, like the organ's swell, where saintliest worlds adore:
"Angel — Darling — let me grasp thee! — Let these arms once, only, clasp thee!"
And with arms outspread and groping, he fell blindly to the floor.

XXIII.

There crept a hush on Nature, and each dumb and browsing creature
Turn'd its head with instinct reverence unto the sacred East;
And midway of the Heaven burst the imperial Star of Even;
For the tyrant Wind was broken, and the Wintry storm had ceased.

XXIV.

The solemn bells were chiming, in a measured cadence timing
All the world's supreme pulsation when there dies Another Day;
And the shining hosts of glory in sweet murmurs told the story
Of our Blessed Saviour's Coming, and the Manger where He lay.

XXV.

The silent moon swept gleaming, 'mid her planet-torches streaming,
And she paved the floor with quaint designs of pearl and silver bands;
But the old man, calmly sleeping, still his Christmas Eve was keeping
Prone in the ghostly radiance, with his face upon his hands.

THE DYING YEAR.

DYING at last, Old Year!
Another stroke of yonder clock, and thou
Wilt pass the threshold of the world we see,
Into the world where Yesterday and Now
Blend with the hours of the No More To Be.

I saw the moon last night
Rise like a crown from the dim mountain's head
And to the Council of the Stars take way;
For thou, the King, though kinsman of the dead,
Sway'd still the sceptre of Another Day.

I see the moon to-night,
Sightless and misty as a mourner's eye
Behind a veil; or, like a coin to seal
The lids of Time's last-born to majesty,
Press'd on the eyes that look a Last Appeal.

Mark where yon shadow crawls
By slow degrees beneath the window-sill,
Timed by the death-watch, ticking slow and dull;
The tide of night is rising, black and still —
Old Year, thou diest when 't is at its full!

Aye! moan and moan again,
And shake all nature in thine agony,
And tear the ermine robes that mock thee now
Like gilded fruit upon a blasted tree ;
To-morrow comes ! To-morrow, where art Thou ?

Would'st thou be shrived, Old Year ?
Thou subtle sentence of delusive Time,
Framed but to deepen all the mystery
Of Life's great purpose ! Come, confess the crime,
And man's Divinity shall date from thee !

Speak to my soul, Old Year ;
Let but a star leave its bright eminence
In thy death struggle, if this deathless Soul
Holds its own destiny and recompense
In the grand mast'ry of a God's control !

No sound, no sign from thee ?
And must I live, not knowing why I live,
Whilst Thou and years to come pass by me here
With faces hid, refusing still to give
The one poor word that bids me cease to fear ?

That word, I charge thee, speak !
Quick ! for the moments tremble on the verge
Of the black chasm where lurks the midnight spell,
And solemn winds already chant thy dirge —
Give Earth its Heav'n, or Hell a deeper Hell !

Speak ! or I curse thee here !
I 'll call it YEA if but a wither'd twig,

Toss'd by the wind, falls rattling on the roof;
I 'll call it YEA, if e'en a shutter creak,
Breathe but on me, and it shall stand for proof!

Too late! The midnight bell —
The crawling shadow at its witching flood,
With the deep gloom of the Beyond is wed,
And I, unanswer'd, sit within and brood,
And thou, Old Year, art silent — Thou art DEAD!

THE LAST DAY.

I.

LIKE some dark Soul whose wearied Passions sleep,
  Yet is itself a watchful, sentient thing,
Poised in the void of Instinct's pulseless Deep,
  Where broods and low'rs, on unascending wing,
A voiceless, vague Eternity of Fear:
  So, looming spectral through a vaster sphere
Of shade all shadowless and crystal clear
  As purpling pallor from a cold, dead Sun; —
Soundless of life, save where a mournful bell
Wails from its cleaving tongue the crooning knell
    Of the last Hour it pealeth: —
  A Nun! In hooded Universe, a Nun,
    The World unbreathing kneeleth.

II.

In awful court the dying Stars look down,
  With something weird and deathful in the light
Pour'd in a livid lustre from the crown
  That binds the arching temples of the night
In pensive beauty, sorrowfully fair;
  And, gazing sadly from their thrones of air,
Seem dimm'd with pitying, and wan with care
  Of some supernal foresight of the heart

Boding of Change ; and heavy with a dread,
Born from the haunted Stillness overhead,
Of a Command to Sever :
To Part ! from Heaven's brotherhood to part !
And shine no more forever.

III.

A drowning Moon in wat'ry distance swims,
As lifeless white — (in fix'd and baleful mien
Glazed into death between encurdled rims) —
As, stark and still, through shoals of Ocean seen
A stony, staring, upturn'd human face :
And, bearing lonely there in shoreless Space
A ghost of continents, — whose dark'ning trace
Turns wrinkled shadows of a pleading frown, —
Deadens to mist ; as though in lost dismay
Of what Creation's lips of ether say,
Stirr'd by a moaning sorrow :
Go down ! all pale with agony go down !
And rise in Blood To-morrow.

IV.

As pass the Hours ; a mute and viewless throng ; —
Each in its birth a world-surrounding Thought ; —
Drawn from about Humanity again,
A blank, unlived infinity of naught,
In silent, ebbing funeral to GOD,
There falleth, muffled, like a ghostly clod
Upon a coffin caverning the sod
And wide and hollow as the palling skies,
Something of Doom ; to paralyze the heart

And make the deepest dreamless Sleeper start, —
  As though the Sentence hearing:
 Arise! ye Dead, from out your graves Arise!
  The End of Time is nearing.

V.

On couch and cot the countless sons of men,
 From palace walls of pictured watchers built
Down to the bare, and rude, and rafter'd den
 Where lives or lurketh Poverty or Guilt,
In mutely mocking self-communion sleep;
 And, wing'd with terror, through their visions sweep,
To make the flesh in clammy horror creep,
 Embodied Monsters of the rising Past,
Direful of Sin; and saying to the Soul, —
In meaning vengeful of a Judgment Scroll
  Writ with a fate infernal: —
 The Last! of all thy nights on earth, the Last!
  Before the Dawn Eternal.

VI.

The purest breast that Virtue holdeth dear,
 And in the noons of Pestilence and Strife
Lulls to a sweet forgetfulness of fear
 With inward murmurs of a Nobler Life
To crown and bless the martyrdom of This,
 In startled tremors owns the dread amiss
Of Night's unfathomable, dark abyss
 Where coming Evil stills the crouching air;
Throbbing with awe of some Approach unknown,
Told to the dreaming Spirit in the tone
  Of its own sightless reading: —

Prepare! To meet thy Judge in clouds, Prepare!
The Cross anew is Bleeding.

VII.

Through hearts of Guile, (whose fitful, stealthy rest
Scarce drops the lid of lithe and tiger guilt
Hot on the eye, from straining socket prest
To catch and glare defiant at the hilt
It knows impatient waits the Slayer's grasp,)
An icy shudder, worming like an asp,
Thrills slowly terrible; with choking gasp
Of fiercest passion, turn'd poltroon to fate
Vision'd in dreams, and dreadful to the thought
As from its own affright the sense it caught
Of a Decree appalling:
Too Late! To flee and hide thyself, Too Late!
The Hand of God is Falling.

VIII.

And over All, — as wane the watches kept
By lonely shades of buried kindred, drawn
Cold from the graves where they so long have slept
To wait and hail the Last, majestic Dawn
That shows them faces well beloved again,
The bending Heaven grows a paling plain
Of Morning colorless; as though a pain
Of dissolution blanch'd its unborn rose;
Clasping the World in cold and ashen rim,
'Till o'er its circled edge, like caldron's brim,
Fire from the nadir flaketh.
It glows! In swiftly deep'ning flush it glows!
The Last, Red Morning breaketh.

IX.

From slumbers troubled unrefresh'd arise
  The Old and Young; in all their souls to feel
Tired of the scenes that meet their heavy eyes,
  And worn and sick with struggles to conceal
The frenzied, vast accusings of their Dreams.
  And half distrustful to their vision seems
The face first greeting them; which answ'ring teems
  With covert doubtings of its Own clear tale.
Speechless are all, and fill'd with vague dismay,
Lest with the op'ning lips the tongue should say,
    As by an instinct bidden: —
  Unveil! Thy self-accusing heart Unveil!
    The Sin no more is hidden.

X.

With looks cast down, and steps to wand'ring bent,
  Each turns from Each, to seek, apart from Men,
Balm for the strange and restless Discontent
  That moves and darkens in his spirit when
He seeming feels a calm, relentless Eye;
  And, glancing listless to the lurid sky,
Is one of Myriads who see on high,
  In one wild Moment's age with terror gray,
Something to craze the naked Soul, and shake
Earth with the shriek their million voices make,
    As from a bursting prison: —
  'T IS DAY! — O, GOD be Merciful — 'T IS DAY!
    AND YET NO SUN HAS RISEN!

SEMPER FIDELIS.

THY face turn on me when I die,
  That, through the shadows dark and chill,
The deep blue Heaven of thine eye,
  May open to my spirit still.

Let others sacrifice in tears
  What pity they may yield to me ;
But be thy look the look of years,
  And steadfast as thy constancy.

O tender look ! O azure calm !
  Thy spell unbroken o'er me keep ;
Still brooding, like a voiceless psalm,
  Above the twilight of my sleep.

And fall so fair on all of earth,
  That in new meaning I may see
The world's unkindness from my birth,
  And love it all in loving thee.

So, in the latest hour I live,
  To feel so much of coming Heav'n,
Shall teach me better to forgive,
  By teaching that I am forgiv'n.

THE VERSE.

WHO hath his birthright in immortal Song,
  To disappointment should be doubly strong;
In him 't is strength to know that man is frail,
And greatness measured by a might to fail.

When, by a lofty inspiration driv'n,
His pen appears the lightning-tongue of Heav'n,
He writes a dream, — and lo! his lines have caught
The shadow only of a dreamer's thought.

To him all nature in the sunshine spread
Reveals a Poem yet divinely dead;
He sees descend through clouds, in summer show'rs,
The souls transparent of the coming flow'rs;

But when his hand, in mood sublime, would fain
Write out the Poem, penn'd in living rain,
All semblance fadeth as the moisture dries,
The rain remaineth only for his eyes.

One Verse alone all Poetry combines,
Its grandeur perfect in four simple lines:
Earth, Air, Fire, Water, or to bless or curse,
Its writer God, its name the Universe!

SATIRES AND BURLESQUES.

A FABLE FOR STRATEGISTS.

THE Animals once, in a classical age,
   Were fill'd with the wildest affright,
Because of a Serpent a hundred feet long,
   That came on a mission of spite,
      One night,
   And stretch'd himself out in their sight.

The donkey, the sloth, the hyena, and bear,
   The foxes, the monkeys, and cows,
Join'd in with the rest of the statelier herd
   In uproars sufficient to rouse
      Bow-wows
   From dogs — and from felines mee-yows.

It chanced that great Jupiter, passing that way,
   Was call'd to the spot by the sound,
And, straightway establishing criers and court,
   He summon'd the creatures he found
      Around,
   Requesting them all to expound.

Old Leo, the Lion, who crouch'd in a bush,
   Too sick and too feeble to roar,

Made bold to explain, in a dignified way,
The very lamentable bore —
And more —
Of having a snake at their door.

"And, old as I am," mutter'd Leo the lame,
"Myself would the reptile defy;
But snakes, as your worship undoubtedly knows,
Require an opponent that 's spry;
And I
Can better devise than apply.

"Permit me to say, that your worship should name
A champion over the rest,
And give unto him, by your magical pow'r,
What weapon he claims is the best
To wrest
The snake from the family nest."

Then Jupiter nodded a mighty assent,
And ask'd, in a thundering key:
"What animal here feeleth competent quite
To conquer the serpent — if he
From me
Can have what he wishes for, free?"

Up spake a young monkey of average size,
With manner peculiarly bold,
"Yon serpent I 'll conquer and drive to the wall
Before he 's another hour old,
All told —
Provided your promise you hold.

"You see that the Serpent's a hundred feet long,
With so many feet to assail,
And what I require to be even with him,
That I in the fight may prevail —
Not fail,
Is fifty more feet to my Tail."

'T was plain, from the look upon Jupiter's face,
He marvell'd that creature so mean
Should push himself forward to hazard the feat,
Where so many nobler were seen;
But e'en
A monkey 's a monkey, I ween.

So, moving his court, with spectators and all,
Quite close to the enemy's land,
Great Jupiter motion'd the MONKEY to take
His place, where he 'd chosen to stand
So grand,
And work out the scheme he had plann'd.

The MONKEY obey'd, with a confident air,
And scarce had he faced at the foe,
When, giving a glance at his flexible TAIL,
He found it beginning to grow,
You know,
For he had bespoken it so.

'Till fully six coils had been added thereto,
He held it in train with a paw;

But then for his strength rather heavy it weigh'd,
And he on the ground let it draw —
O law!
Such TAIL mortal man never saw.

To fifty full feet it extended at last,
All curl'd on the earth in a pile;
And there was the *Serpent*, and here was his foe,
Both staring in comical style
The while,
As though 't were a joke to beguile.

The MONKEY he chatter'd, the MONKEY he fuss'd,
When Jupiter thunder'd — "Begin!"
But there was the SERPENT, and here was his foe,
With hiss making answer to grin —
As in
Such manner each reckon'd to win.

The animals titter'd, the animals growl'd,
And even the birds in the tree
Alternately croaked with impatience of note,
And chirp'd in the greatest of glee
To see
How comic 't was getting to be.

Great Jupiter frown'd at the battle's delay,
And thunder'd "Begin!" as before.
But there was the SERPENT, and here was his foe,
Each eying the other one o'er,
And o'er,
And — not doing anything more.

The MONKEY he started, the MONKEY fell back,
His TAIL was too heavy to drag;
He lifted a number of coils in his arms,
And struggled along, with a fag
And lag
As limp as an overwash'd rag.

The venomous SERPENT, still eying his foe,
Began to curl up from behind,
And backed jump'd the monkey, entangled in TAIL,
And chatter'd, "O Jupiter kind,
I find
More TAIL I must have to unwind!"

Now Jupiter saw, and the Animals too,
He could n't use all that he had;
But, willing to humor his champion still,
Proceeded, with feelings half glad,
Half mad,
Ten feet to the fifty to add.

The MONKEY he loaded his shoulders with coil,
And painfully started anew;
Yet such was the weight of the pile on the ground,
He stopp'd ere he 'd gone inches two,
And threw
His coils, like a Texan lassoo.

The SERPENT, still keeping an eye on his foe,
Sway'd cunningly backward a bit;

And back hopp'd the MONKEY, entangled in Tail,
Scarce knowing if he 'd made a hit
With it,
And frighten'd half into a fit.

The Animals titter'd, the Animals growl'd,
And Jupiter thunder'd, "Explain!"
"Indeed," sigh'd the MONKEY, "that Snake is so long,
To equal his strength in the main,
'T is plain
A little more Tail I must gain!"

Though Jupiter saw, and the Animals too,
Already it mock'd his control,
He added full twenty more feet to the TAIL,
That mounted immensely in scroll
On scroll,
A hopelessly complicate whole.

The Monkey he loaded his shoulders with coils,
With others his body he wound;
But scarce had he lifted his foot for a step,
When down they all fell on the ground
Around,
In snarls and confusion profound.

The SERPENT, still keeping an eye on his foe,
Indulged in an ominous snap;
And loud scream'd the MONKEY, entangled in TAIL,

"I 've met with a grievous mishap,"
Poor chap —
To fancy a serpent would nap!

The Animals titter'd, the Animals growl'd,
And Jupiter threaten'd a breeze.
"You see," said the MONKEY, "so long is the Snake,
He reaches beyond me to seize —
With ease —
A little more TAIL, if you please!"

Though Jupiter's patience is that of a god,
'T was now very nearly worn out,
Yet waved he the signal, thrice given before,
And twenty more feet, with a flout
About,
Were join'd to the **TAIL** at a sprout.

The *Monkey* he gazed at the mountain of coils
So wond'rously changing his base,
Then wildly and frantic'ly twisted and tugg'd,
To tumble it over the place,
Apace,
Where hiss'd the old Snake in his face.

And vainly he strove; for the mountain of coils
Not only resisted him quite,
But firmly it held him enchain'd to the spot,
And on came the **SERPENT** to bite
The wight
That took so much **TAIL** for a fight!

The monkey he gibber'd, the monkey he shriek'd,
  In fear of a horrible fate —
"O Jupiter, what 's to become of me now? —
  O mercy! don't ponder and wait
      Too late,
  Or I shall be murder'd and ate!"

A nod from the god, and a magical axe
  One moment was seen in the air,
Then straight at the root of the wonderful **TAIL**
  It flew — and the *Monkey* was bare
      Of e'er
  The least bit of tail he could wear!

And just at the moment this thing was achieved,
  The *Serpent*, with croak like a frog,
Went off through the bushes, but left in his trail
  Full half of his length in the bog —
      A log,
  With which he 'd pretended to jog!

The Animals titter'd, the Animals growl'd,
  The *Monkey* look'd crush'd and forlorn!
'T was plain, from his bitter expression of face,
  He wish'd that he 'd never been born;
      Nor shorn
  Of what he so proudly had worn.

Then silence was order'd, and Jupiter turn'd.
  And unto the *Monkey* said he:

"I gave you your way, and a very nice way
  That way has been proved unto me
            To be,
  And ends — as we all of us see!

"Since you 're but a *monkey*, my sentence is light:
  Go back to your kindred and friends,
And possibly you for a hero may pass —
  As one who, to make his amends,
            Pretends
  The gods have defeated his ends!"

The Animals, struck with a sentence so just,
  To Jupiter raised an All Hail!
And cherish'd the lesson, that ever it lies
  In length of the head to prevail —
            Not fail —
  And not in the length of the tail.

BYRON CHOLER.

AY, but the moon was afraid that night,
  Paler than ever you see her now ;
Glazed like an eye at a ghostly sight,
  Crown'd with a cloud like a shaggy brow.

Sinister e'en was the gleam she threw
  Over the carpet there at my feet,
When, from my bosom, my own wife flew,
  Out of the window, into the street.

Was there a sound on the walk below?
  Were there some pieces pick'd up next morn?
How in my slumber was I to know?
  Innocent I as the babe unborn.

Yes, it is said that my tears were few ;
  Said that I whistled and sang that week ·
Let them believe if they think it true,
  Little care I for the words they speak.

Both of my parents who died, you say,
  Carried blue finger-marks 'neath their chins :
Well, there are some who *will* die that way :
  Heaven have mercy for all their sins !

Bah! do you think I would fear a ghost?
  One there is with me half of the time:
'T is but a trick of the eye, at most, —
  Holding the tableau after the crime.

O, what a spectre Girletta makes,
  Clad in the daintiest, best of palls!
Pretty as ever, her head she shakes;
  Pity she slipt that night at the Falls!

True, there are others to win my love,
  Such as the wife of my dearest friend:
Strange he should start for the realms above,
  After the wine I was ask'd to send!

Accidents happen to one and all:
  Think of my little one, angel Jim!
Why should my gun have been left at all,
  Loaded and capp'd, in the reach of him?

Well, I can scorn what the world may say,
  I am above it so high and far;
All of the spots they would charge my ray,
  Lurk in the telescope, not the star.

Yet there 's a grief at my bosom's core,
  Dwindling my life to a smaller span;
Earth unto me can be bright no more, —
  Some one has stolen my black-and-tan!

THE HAIRESS.

I.

IN Rutgers' halls a maid I knew,
  With her hair unbecomingly dress'd;
She 'd lips of red and eyes of blue,
  With her hair unbecomingly dress'd;
Such a taper waist and a lovely arm
And shoulders white were enough to charm
The sourest saint and his heart alarm —
  With her hair unbecomingly dress'd.

II.

She had a brow of Grecian mould,
  With her hair unbecomingly dress'd;
The nose that Venus wore of old,
  With her hair unbecomingly dress'd;
Her rosy mouth was a kiss divine,
Preserved, as 't were, in a ruby wine,
Through which its sweets, to tempt, might shine —
  With her hair unbecomingly dress'd.

III.

She sat upon the scholar's bench,
  With her hair unbecomingly dress'd,

To study music, Greek, and French,
  With her hair unbecomingly dress'd ;
She flirted with Signor Shaykantrill,
Who taught her opera and quadrille,
And managed of novels to read her fill,
  With her hair unbecomingly dress'd.

IV.

They took her from the boarding-school,
  With her hair unbecomingly dress'd ;
And had her robed in silk and tulle,
  With her hair unbecomingly dress'd.
She entered society's bright pell-mell,
And took the palm of the reigning belle,
And cast upon ev'ry heart a spell,
  With her hair unbecomingly dress'd.

V.

She drove a phaeton in the Park,
  With her hair unbecomingly dress'd ;
Came back to dinner just at dark,
  With her hair unbecomingly dress'd.
She went to the matinée, ball, and rout,
To dance, to simper, to smile, and pout ;
And then to the Springs when the ton went out,
  With her hair unbecomingly dress'd.

VI.

Not long had such a nymph to wait,
  With her hair unbecomingly dress'd,
For one to be her lord and mate,
  With her hair unbecomingly dress'd.

'T was the son of a heavy dry-goods man .
One night at a hop pick'd up her fan ;
And she promised to share his heart and span,
  With her hair unbecomingly dress'd.

VII.

Return'd to town an autumn-bride,
  With her hair unbecomingly dress'd,
She took a coach, and Ma inside,
  With her hair unbecomingly dress'd ;
Went straight to Stewart's to buy the things
That women wear in the place of wings,
And order'd of Tiffany pearls by strings,
  With her hair unbecomingly dress'd.

VIII.

She had a wedding *à la mode*,
  With her hair unbecomingly dress'd ;
And then to Jersey Ferry road,
  With her hair unbecomingly dress'd ;
For Washington City they took the train,
Where the honeymoon should wax and wane,
And over the rails she sped amain,
  With her hair unbecomingly dress'd.

IX.

The nation's wisdom greeted her,
  With her hair unbecomingly dress'd ;
She made the season all astir,
  With her hair unbecomingly dress'd ;

She flirted with Senators sharp and snub,
While her liege and lord was at the club,
And shone supreme at dance and rub,
  With her hair unbecomingly dress'd.

X.

Her husband saw her doing thus,
  With her hair unbecomingly dress'd;
She begg'd him not to make a fuss,
  With her hair unbecomingly dress'd;
But he was resolved on a homeward trip,
And little he heeded her pouting lip,
And home she came in his bearish grip,
  With her hair unbecomingly dress'd.

XI.

Upon the train she felt a chill,
  With her hair unbecomingly dress'd;
It made her quickly very ill,
  With her hair unbecomingly dress'd;
The bonnet she wore was so very small
That it scarcely seem'd a bonnet at all;
And how could she cover her head in a shawl,
  With her hair unbecomingly dress'd?

XII.

Arrived in town she went to bed,
  With her hair unbecomingly dress'd;
And cough'd enough to split her head,
  With her hair unbecomingly dress'd;

The doctors came in a stately host,
And with powder and pill the patient dosed ;
But in less than a week she became a ghost,
  With her hair unbecomingly dress'd.

XIII.

In garments rich she slept her last,
  With her hair unbecomingly dress'd ;
And to a better world had pass'd,
  With her hair unbecomingly dress'd ;
Where the snow melts first in the breath of spring
And the sweetest birds the latest sing,
She waits the great awakening,
  With her hair unbecomingly dress'd !

ADVICE TO A MAID.

BY AN OLD BACHELOR.

PERENNIAL maiden, thou art no less fair
Than those whose fairness barely equals thine ;
And like a cloud on Athos is thy hair,
Touch'd with Promethean fire to make it shine
Above the temple of a soul divine ;
And yet, methinks, it doth resemble, too,
The strands Berenice 'mid the stars doth twine,
As Mitchell's small Astronomy doth show ;
Procure the book, dear maid, when to the town you go.

Young as thou art, thou might'st be younger still,
If divers years were taken from thy life :
And who shall say, if marry man thou will,
Thou may'st not prove some man's own wedded wife ?
Such things do happen in this worldly strife,
If they take place — that is, if they are done ;
For with warm love this earthly dream is rife —
And where love shines there always is a sun —
That is, if shadows sombre rest not thereupon.

Supposing thou dost marry, thou wilt yearn
For that which thou dost want ; in fact, desire —

The wisdom shaped for older heads to learn,
And well design'd to tame Youth's giddy fire :
The wisdom, conflicts with the world inspire,
Such as, perchance, I may myself possess,
Though I am but a man, as was my sire,
And own not wisdom such as gods may bless ;
For man is only naught, and naught is nothingness.

Still, I may tell thee all that I do know,
And, telling that, tell all I comprehend ;
Since all man hath is all that he can show,
And what he hath not, is not his to lend.
Therefore, young maid, if you will but attend,
You shall hear that which shall salute your ear ;
But if you list not, I my breath shall spend
Upon the zephyrs wandering there and here,
The far-off hearing less, perhaps, than those more near.

Remember this : thou art thy husband's wife,
And he the mortal thou art married to ;
Else thou fore'er hadst led a single life,
And he had never come thy heart to woo.
Rememb'ring this, do thou remember, too,
He is thy bridegroom, thou his chosen bride;
And if unto his side thou provest true,
Then thou wilt be forever at his side ;
As Tacitus observes, with some degree of pride.

See that his buttons to his shirts adhere,
As Trojan Hector to the walls of Troy ;
And see that not, Achilles-like, appear
Rents in his stocking-heels ; but be your joy

To have his wardrobe all your thoughts employ,
Save such deep thought as may, in duty giv'n,
Suit to his tastes his dinners; nor annoy
Digestion's tenor in its progress even;
Then his the joy of Harvard, Boston, and high Heav'n.

If a bread-pudding thou wouldst fondly make —
A thing nutritious, but no costly meal —
Of bread that 's stale a due proportion take,
And soak in water warm enough to feel;
Then add a strip or two of lemon-peel,
With curdled milk and raisins to your taste,
And stir the whole with ordinary zeal,
Until the mass becomes a luscious paste.
Such pudding strengthens man, and doth involve no
waste.

See thou thy husband's feet are never wet —
For wet brings cold, and colds such direful aches
As old Parrhasius never felt when set
On cruel racks or slow impaling stakes.
Make him abstain, if sick, from griddle-cakes —
They, being rich, his stomach might derange —
And if in thin-soled shoes a walk he takes,
See that his stockings he doth quickly change.
Thus should thy woman's love through woman's duties
range.

And now, fair maiden, all the stars grow pale,
And teeming Nature drinks the morning dews;
And I must hasten to my Orient vale,
And quick put on a pair of over-shoes.

If from my words your woman's heart may choose
To find a guidance for a future way,
The Olympian impulse and the lyric muse
In such approval shall accept their pay.
And so, good day, young girl — ah me! O my! good day.

THE REJECTED "NATIONAL HYMNS."

NATIONAL HYMN.

BY H——Y W. L–NGF——W.

BACK in the years when Phlagstaff, the Dane, was monarch
Over the sea-ribb'd land of the fleet-footed Norsemen,
Once there went forth young Ursa to gaze at the heavens —
Ursa, the noblest of all the Vikings and horsemen.

Musing, he sat in his stirrups and viewed the horizon,
Where the Aurora lapt stars in a North-polar manner,
Wildly he started, — for there in the heavens before him
Flutter'd and flam'd the original Star-Spangled Banner.

NATIONAL HYMN.

BY THE HON. CH——S S–MN–R.

POND'ROUS projectiles, hurl'd by heavy hands,
Fell on our Liberty's poor infant head,
Ere she a stadium had well advanced

K

On the great path that to her greatness led;
Her temple's propylon was shatterèd;
Yet, thanks to saving Grace and Washington,
Her incubus was from her bosom hurl'd;
And, rising like a cloud-dispelling sun,
She took the oil with which her hair was curl'd
To grease the "Hub" round which revolves the world.

NATIONAL HYMN.

BY J-HN GR—NL—F WH—T—R.

My Native Land, thy Puritanic stock
Still finds its roots firm-bound in Plymouth Rock,
And all thy sons unite in one grand wish —
To keep the virtues of Preservèd Fish.

Preservèd Fish, the Deacon stern and true,
Told our New England what her sons should do,
And if they swerve from loyalty and right,
Then the whole land is lost indeed in night.

NATIONAL HYMN.

BY DR. OL-V-R W-ND—L H-LMES.

A diagnosis of our hist'ry proves
Our native land a land its native loves;
Its birth a deed obstetric without peer,
Its growth a source of wonder far and near.

To love it more behold how foreign shores
Sink into nothingness beside its stores;
Hyde Park at best — though counted ultra-grand —
The "Boston Common" of Victoria's land —

NATIONAL HYMN.

BY R-LPH W-LDO EM-R—N.

SOURCE immaterial of material naught,
Focus of light infinitesimal,
Sum of all things by sleepless Nature wrought,
Of which the normal man is decimal.

Refract, in prism immortal, from thy stars
To the stars blent incipient on our flag,
The beam translucent, neutrifying death;
And raise to immortality the rag.

NATIONAL HYMN.

BY W-LL—M C-LL-N B-Y-NT.

THE sun sinks softly to his ev'ning post,
The sun swells grandly to his morning crown;
Yet not a star our Flag of Heav'n has lost,
And not a sunset stripe with him goes down.

So thrones may fall, and from the dust of those
New thrones may rise, to totter like the last;
But still our Country's nobler planet glows
While the eternal stars of Heaven are fast.

NATIONAL HYMN.

BY G—RGE P. M–RR–S.

IN the days that tried our fathers,
  Many years ago,
Our fair land achieved her freedom,
  Blood-bought, you know.
Shall we not defend her ever
  As we 'd defend
That fair maiden, kind and tender,
  Calling us friend?

Yes! Let all the echoes answer,
  From hill and vale;
Yes! Let other nations, hearing,
  Joy in the tale.
Our Columbia is a lady,
  High-born and fair;
We have sworn allegiance to her —
  Touch her who dare.

NATIONAL HYMN.

BY N. P. W–LL–S.

ONE hue of our Flag is taken
  From the cheeks of my blushing Pet.
And its stars beat time and sparkle
  Like the studs on her chemisette.

Its blue is the ocean shadow
  That hides in her dreamy eyes,
It conquers all men, like her,
  And still for a Union flies.

NATIONAL HYMN.

BY TH–M–S B–IL–Y ALD—CH.

The little brown squirrel hops in the corn,
  The cricket quaintly sings,
The emerald pigeon nods his head,
  And the shad in the river springs,
The dainty sunflow'r hangs its head
  On the shore of the summer sea;
And better far that I were dead,
  If Maud did not love me.

I love the squirrel that hops in the corn,
  And the cricket that quaintly sings;
And the emerald pigeon that nods his head,
  And the shad that gayly springs.
I love the dainty sunflow'r, too,
  And Maud with her snowy breast;
I love them all;—but I love—I love—
  I love my country best.

NATIONAL HYMN.

BY R. H. ST–D—RD.

Behold the flag! Is it not a flag?
  Deny it, man, if you dare;

And midway spread, 'twixt earth and sky,
  It hangs like a written pray'r.

Would impious hand of foe disturb
  Its memories' holy spell,
And blight it with a dew of blood?
  Ha, tr-r-aitor!! . . . . It is well.

AGE BLUNTLY CONSIDERED.

AS Age advances, ails and aches attend,
 Backs builded broadest burdensomely bend;
Cuttingly cruel comes consuming Care,
Dealing delusions, drivelry, despair.

Empty endeavor enervately ends,
Fancy forlornly feigns forgotten friends;
Gout, grimly griping, gluttonously great,
Hastens humanity's hard-hearted hate.

Intentions imbecile invent ideas
Justly jocunding jolly jokers' jeers;
Knowledge — keen kingdom knurlyably known —
Lingers, lamenting life's long lasting loan.

Mammonly mumming, magnifying motes,
Nurtures numb Nature's narrowest nursery notes,
Opens old Ogre's odious offering out —
Peevish punctilio, parrot-pining pout.

Qualmishly querying, quarrelsomely quaint,
Rousing rife ridicule's repeal'd restraint;
Speaking soft silliness — such shallow show,
That tottering toysters, tickled, titter too.

Useless, ungainly, unbelov'd, unblest,
Virtue's vague visor, vice's veiling vest,
Wheezingly whimpering, wanting wisdom, wit,
'Xistence, 'Xigeñt, 'Xclaims — 'Xit!

Youths, you 're yclept youth's youngest; yet you 'll
yield
Zestless zig-zaggers, zanyable zeal'd.

QUE VOULEZ-VOUS?

ATTEND, thou lively son of Gaul,
  And lay thy skillet by;
The dainty omelet can wait,
  While counsel thou and I
Upon the sinister events
  Producing such mischance
As, in a round of ruin, binds
  The hapless land of France.

Nor let thy shoulders rise and fall
  In such a specious shrug,
Which meaneth what begins with "hum"
  And endeth with a "bug";
For, though American, I have
  No Office tempting me,
And, needing not the German vote,
  Give France my sympathy.

Whence is it that the land of arms,
  Of chivalry and song,
That, shining like a Knight in mail,
  Has awed the world so long, —
From daring Prussia to the lists,
  With trump and bugle trill,

Now trembles vanquished at the feet
  Of pious Kaiser Bill?

Whence is it? — O my brother Gaul,
  Inform me! — Can it be
Thy nation comes to this at last
  By ceasing to be Free!
By e'en preferring peace and wealth
  Beneath an Empire's yoke,
To patriot-fighting ev'ry day
  For Liberty dead-broke?

Or comes this dread defeat to her
  Retributive, because
She, in her gay career, forgot
  The graver moral laws,
And, in her Capital's display
  Of aggravating mirth,
Gave scandal to each smaller town,
  And duller, too, on earth?

Or is it — ah, perhaps it is! —
  By reason of the Sin
That left the Pope without a guard,
  And let King Victor in;
That, calling back her troops from Rome,
  Left Rome as much a chance
To choose a ruler for herself
  As though she were in France?

No answer yet thou givest me;
  But read I in thy face,

There may be other reasons still
  For Gaul's supreme disgrace !
Was it her people's ignorance,
  That fated her to find
In German arms the mastery
  First found in German Mind ?

O fellow-man, confide in me !
  And tell me, as a friend,
If one or all these causes named
  Brought on this bitter end ?
So shall thy modest name be known
  As that of honor'd sage,
Whose subtle wisdom solved the great
  Conundrum of the age !

Then look'd that lively son of Gaul
  Most keenly all around,
And softly went and closed the door
  With secrecy profound ;
And whispered sharply in mine ear,
  In quite a candid way :
" Ze raison vy ze French get vip,
  Is — 'cause zey run avay ! "

DYING OUT.

'TWAS by the wayside, near a Southern town,
  I spied a sage beneath a tree reclining;
His old straw hat was guiltless of a crown,
  His pantaloons had less of cloth than lining.
Addressing him about the latest news,
  I quickly found him, by his answer hazy,
A man of pow'rful and elaborate views,
  And gifts of reasoning to make you crazy.

"I reckon you 're a Yankee, come," said he,
  "Upon some sneaking mission or another,
To see how being Equalized and Free
  Agrees with him you call your Color'd Brother.
Extinction waits on him, with all his Rights
  So freely given by your laws confounded!
He 'll keep attacking the defenceless Whites
  Till all the Color'd race are kill'd or wounded.

"In New Orleans — behold the lesson taught! —
  When in Convention certain Blacks assembled,
A sound of peaceful throngs outside was caught,
  And in the hall the Blacks bloodthirsty trembled.
Then through the windows, lobbies, outer gate,
  By the unarm'd Caucasian race surrounded,

The Freedmen sallied in their murd'rous hate,
  And nineteen Color'd men were badly wounded.

"In Central Georgia, sev'ral months ago,
  The sons of Afric held a Loyal meeting,
And divers White Men went to see the show,
  And give the speakers friendly Southern greeting.
But lo! when speaking had gone on a spell,
  And all the air with loyal words resounded,
Upon the Whites, like fiends, the Negroes fell,
  And thirteen Color'd men were badly wounded.

"In old Virginia, at a rural place,
  Where many Africans had come for voting,
The merest handful of the Higher Race
  Were looking on, and minor matters noting;
When, at a cry about some vote refused,
  The Blacks, infuriate, on the handful bounded,
Their knives and pistols mercilessly used,
  And fourteen Color'd men were badly wounded.

"So, at the Capital of all the States —
  Your boasted Washington, the placid city —
There was, in journals of the proper dates,
  Correct report of what should move your pity:
The town election rallied countless Blacks,
  Who, arm'd and madden'd, and to riot hounded,
Upon the helpless White men made attacks,
  And fifteen Color'd men were badly wounded.

"Yet furthermore: of late, in Tennessee,
  Where Stokes was beaten at the polls by Senter,

The savage Negroes, arm'd from head to knee,
  Seem'd on a fight than on their votes intenter;
To vent some petty, diabolic spite,
  Upon the plea of some vague charge unfounded,
They turn'd in fury on a single White,
  And sixteen Color'd men were badly wounded.

"The race of Color'd men is Dying Out!"
  The sage concluded, with a dismal gesture;
And left me victim of amazing doubt,
  While he went onward in his ragged vesture.
I 'd often heard his mournful last remark,
  When used by Southern politicians, merely
To hint the Freedman's future lot was dark, —
  But not till then had understood it clearly!

THE AMERICAN TRAVELLER.

TO Lake Aghmoogenegamook,
  All in the State of Maine,
A man from Wittequergaugaum came
  One evening in the rain.

"I am a traveller," said he,
  "Just started on a tour,
And go to Nomjamskillicook
  To-morrow morn at four."

He took a tavern bed that night,
  And with the morrow's sun,
By way of Sekledobskus went,
  With carpet-bag and gun.

A week pass'd on; and next we find
  Our native tourist come
To that sequester'd village call'd
  Genasagarnagum.

From thence he went to Absequoit,
  And there — quite tired of Maine —
He sought the mountains of Vermont,
  Upon a railroad train.

Dog Hollow, in the Green Mount State,
  Was his first stopping-place,
And then Skunk's Misery display'd
  Its sweetness and its grace.

By easy stages then he went
  To visit Devil's Den;
And Scrabble Hollow, by the way,
  Did come within his ken.

Then, *via* Nine Holes and Goose Green
  He travell'd through the State,
And to Virginia, finally,
  Was guided by his fate.

Within the Old Dominion's bounds
  He wandered up and down;
To-day, at Buzzard Roost ensconced,
  To-morrow, at Hell Town.

At Pole Cat, too, he spent a week,
  Till friends from Bull Ring came,
nd made him spend a day with them
  In hunting forest game.

Then, with his carpet-bag in hand,
  To Dog Town next he went;
Though stopping at Free Negro Town,
  Where half a day he spent.

From thence, into Negationburg
  His route of travel lay,

Which having gain'd, he left the State
  And took a southward way.

North Carolina's friendly soil
  He trod at fall of night,
And, on a bed of softest down,
  He slept at Hell's Delight.

Morn found him on the road again,
  To Lazy Level bound ;
At Bull's Tail, and Lick Lizzard, too,
  Good provender he found.

But the plantations near Burnt Coat
  Were even finer still,
And made the wond'ring tourist feel
  A soft, delicious thrill.

At Tear Shirt, too, the scenery
  Most charming did appear,
With Snatch It in the distance far,
  And Purgatory near.

But, 'spite of all these pleasant scenes,
  The tourist stoutly swore,
That home is brightest, after all,
  And travel is a bore.

So back he went to Maine, straightway,
  A little wife he took ;
And now is making nutmegs at
  Moosehicmaguntìcook.

THE MAUDLIN MUSE.

O my little Maud is a dainty queen,
  With quaint and tiny shoon,
And her cheek is red as a baton rouge ;
  And her eye is the full-blown moon.

And O, I love my own little Maud,
  As the petrel loves the sea,
And I should die like a penguin pale
  If Maud did not love me.

In Spring's first blush I met little Maud,
  When the time of year was glad,
And the flounder flash'd on the ocean wave,
  And the low of the kine was sad.

The quaint little bugs wove nets of gauze
  To snare the dainty bee,
And the lily droop'd its bald white head
  And sigh'd " Ah ! woe is me ! "

The Junebug pick'd his felt guitar,
  And the swallows swarm'd with bliss,
When I met Maud at the castle gate—
  O, sair such a world as this ! —

When I met Maud at the castle gate,
  With a tear in either eye,
And swore by the red, red moon above
  To love till I die — I die.

The churchyard pheasant heard my oath,
  As he scratch'd his downy head,
And the indigo pigeon began to hop,
  And hopp'd till he was dead.

The stars look'd down on the sobbing world,
  With a quaintness all their own,
But Maud and I were too blest for speech,
  For our love had a silent tone.

I cover'd her up with the kiss I gave,
  I kiss'd her there, I swear ;
And the moon went under a ghostly cloud,
  And the moon it dazed me sair.

'T were well we met that time, little Maud,
  'T were well we 'd died there, too ;
For I mark'd, as I went, the cow's low call,
  And the faint magnolia's hue.

The snake look'd up as I went, little Maud,
  The snake with the hood of black,
And I heard him say to the shining eel,
  " Alack ! alack ! alack ! "

I heard him say to the flashing eel,
  Far down in the mosses gray,

"This love's to-morrow never comes
  Till to-day is yesterday."

The hoptoad raised his eye of fire
  And look'd at the anguish'd sky,
And the harebell's sigh I 'll ne'er forget
  Till I die — I die — I die.

O, weep, and weep, and weep, little Maud,
  Like a saucer brimming o'er,
For the time that came and the time that went,
  And cometh nevermore.

The moonbeam glints on the dainty crag,
  And the porpoise skims the sea;
But who shall glide to the maid I love,
  That waits so long for me?

O, who shall glide to the maid I love,
  And sob in her gentle ear,
That the small brown rabbits moan her name,
  And the reed-bird sheds a tear?

I wait thee here at the stile, my love,
  With the splashy stars abroad,
And my heart goes out with a gush to thee,
  Little Maud! little Maud! little Maud!

WOMAN'S HEART.

BY SAIRA NEVERMAIR.

WE went to the world-loved Ball last night,
  Claude and I, in our robes of gold;
He in a coat as black as jet,
  And I in the jewels I wore of old.

Diamonds cover'd my head in pounds,
  Seventy large ones lit my neck, —
Over my skirts they burn'd in quarts
  Counting in all a goodly peck.

Hopp'd the canary 'neath the wires, —
  Spoke the canary not a word;
When to my heart the chill has struck,
  How can I sing? — can e'er a bird?

We were together, Claude and I,
  Bonded together as man and wife;
Little I thought, as I utter'd my vows,
  What was the real Ideal of life.

He is my Husband to love and obey, —
  Those were the words of the priest, I think, —
He is to purchase the clothes I wear,
  Order my victuals and order my drink!

Well, it is well if it must be so :
  Woman the slave and man the lord ;
She the scissors to cut the threads
  After the darning, and he the sword.

Was it for this I play'd my cards,
  Tuned the piano's tender din,
Cherish'd a delicate health, and ate
  Pickles and pencils to make me thin ?

Better it were to be born a serf,
  Holding a soul by a master's lease ;
Better than learning Society's law,
  Gaining a Husband and forfeiting peace.

Mortimer sighs as he sees me dance,
  Percy is sad as he passes by,
Herbert turns pallid beneath my glance ;
  All of them married — and so am I.

Well, if the world must have it so,
  Woman can only stand and endure ;
Ever the grossness of all that is gross
  Rises the tyrant of all that is pure.

Marriage, they say, is a sacred thing ;
  So is the fetter that yields a smart :
Give *one* crumb to the starving wretch,
  And give *one* Object to Woman's Heart.

Claude, they tell me, should own my love ;
  Well, I have loved him nearly a week ;

Looking at one man longer than that
  Grows to be tiresome — so to speak.

What if he calls me Angel wife;
  Angels are not for the One to win;
Yet is my passionate love like theirs, —
  Theirs is a love taking all men in.

Hops the canary 'neath the wires,
  Speaks the canary not a word;
When to my heart the chill has struck,
  How can I sing? — can e'er a bird?

COLUMBIA'S AGONY. (1862.)

BY MARTIN FARQUHAR TUP—R.

I HOLD it good — as who shall hold it bad?
  To lave Columbia in the boiling tears
I shed for Freedom when my soul is sad,
  And having shed proceed to shed again:
For *human sadness sad to all appears*,
  And tears men sometimes shed are shed by men.

The normal nation lives until it dies,
  As men may die when they have ceased to live;
But when abnormal, by a foe's surprise,
  It may not reach its first-appointed goal;
For *what we have not is not ours to give*,
  And if we miss it all we miss the whole.

Columbia, young, a giant baby born,
  Aim'd at a manhood ere the child had been,
And, slipping downward in a strut forlorn,
  Learns, to its sorrow, what 't is good to know,
That *babes who walk too soon, too soon begin*
  To walk, in this dark vale of life below.

When first the State of Charleston did secede,
  And Morrill's tariff was declared repeal'd,

The soul of Freedom ev'rywhere did bleed
For that which, having seen, it sadly saw;
So true it is, *death wounds are never heal'd,*
And law defied is not unquestion'd law.

The mother-poet, England, sadly view'd
The strife unnatural across the wave,
And with maternal tenderness renew'd
Her sweet assurances of neutral love;
A mother's love may not its offspring save;
But mother's love is still a mother's love.

Learn thou, Columbia, in thine agony,
That England loves thee, with a love as deep
As my "Proverbial Philosophy"
Has won for me from her approving breast;
The love that never slumbers cannot sleep,
And all for highest good is for the best.

Thy Freedom fattens on the work of slaves,
Her Grace of Sutherland informeth me;
And all thy South Amboy is full of graves,
Where tortured bondmen snatch a dread repose;
Learn, then, *the race enslaved is never free,*
And in thy woes incurr'd, behold thy woes.

Thy pride is humbled, humbled is thy pride,
And now misfortunes come upon thee, thick
With dark reproaches for the right defied,
And cloud thy banner in a dim eclipse;
Sic transit gloria, gloria transit sic,
The mouth that speaketh useth its own lips.

Thus speeds the world, and thus our planet speeds ;
  What is, must be ; and what can't be, is not ;
Our acts unwise are not our wisest deeds,
  And what we do is what ourselves have done ;
Mistakes remember'd are not faults forgot,
  And we must wait for day to see the sun.

"TRUE STORY."

BY MRS. H——T B—CH–R ST–WE

IN a village of New England, at the closing of the day,
Stood a youth of feeble aspect all upon the broad highway;
And he wept with so much fervor, and so wretched did appear,
That the Oldtown Folks, beholding, in their pity, ventured near.

Soon an old man of the village — Uncle Tom his honor'd name —
Placed a hand upon the shoulder of that bending human frame;
And, in accents low and kindly as the voice of age can come,
Ask'd the stranger why he sorrow'd all so far from Hearth and Home.

Was he mourning that his kindred were all gather'd to the dead?
Was he weeping that his fellows would not give him work or bread?

Was he sad from weary waiting for the helping hand
of man ?
Was the falsehood of a woman what had made him
weak and wan ?

"None of these," the stranger answer'd, "made me
what you here behold,
I 'm not thirsty, nor a-hunger'd ; I 'm not wearied nor
a-cold ;
But I 'm madden'd with the knowledge just become
for me extant
That my Father is my Uncle and my Mother is my
Aunt !"

A TRUCE.

THE Southern hosts are up in arms!
The olive-branch no longer charms,
And over cities, prairies, farms,
The martial trumpet rings.
A single spark has lit the North,
Her sons of valor hurry forth,
And, with a soldier's spirit wroth,
Each man to harness springs.

From East to West the cry has gone:
The pledge is broke, the sword is drawn,
And now the moment dread comes on,
That all our honor proves.
A score of millions hear the cry;
Six hundred thousand, marching by,
Give back, in thunder tones, reply:
Our banner southward moves!

Then pours the hurrying tide of war,
The billowy smoke, the cannon's roar,
The bayonet's lightning-flash before,
The Standard's sunset glow;
And over all the tumult comes
The trumpet's bray, the roll of drums;

While, from the lowland distance hums
The echo of the foe.

Blow, bugles, blow! the charge begins;
Now God uphold the arm that wins,
And look with mercy on the sins
Of those who fall to-day;
A glorious stake is in the fight,
A nation's life, a nation's right;
And where her champions' blows alight,
There let the vanquish'd pray!

A sudden pause, a sudden hush;
The mighty boulder, launch'd to crush
Hangs, like a feather on a bush,
In fathomless suspense;
As though an avalanche, half hurl'd
Upon a nether Alpine world,
Were caught, where first it downward swirl'd,
Upon a saving fence!

In mid career the armies stand,
Each by the other's breathing fann'd,
While all around them smokes the land
Their iron heels have trod.
The gunner's lanyard slacken'd droops,
The horseman to his sabre stoops,
The hostile captains eye their troops,
With many a thoughtful nod.

To this the strife has come at last,
That, in the texture of the blast,

A mighty flaw should overcast
The rushing Ship of State,
And hold her in a leaden calm,
While her defenders found the balm
To keep her safe from ev'ry harm,
Or else, defer her fate.

Deep quiet reigns along the lines,
The midnight frowns, the noonday shines;
But still Bellona's great designs
Are left to other men;
For, in a field where gods might choose
To sip the fountains of the dews,
The Brigadiers, in fearless crews,
Renew the strife again.

They meet the foemen face to face —
Who loses now shall win disgrace;
For on his strength to keep his place
His land's salvation hangs! —
They scan each other through the glass,
From rank to rank the watchwords pass,
Then, pressing forward in a mass,
The goblet mortar clangs!

"Load up with bricks!" the leader said,
Ere half the earliest round had sped,
"And truly aim at every head
Above the table-land."
Their duty well the gunners know,
The volley'd corks at angles go,
And pours the grape with such a flow
No mortal man can stand.

Lo! Sherry flashes to the front,
With Bourbon's self to share the brunt,
And valiant Southside, old and blunt,
  Stands out to meet them there.
Now hasten! hasten while ye can,
Old burly, clumsy Rhenish man;
For Heidsick comes to lead the van,
  And falter then who dare!

Cabaña's battery 's in reserve,
With steady fire our charge to nerve;
Who would a coward be, and swerve
  Before the lighted match?
Already reels the foe, struck dumb,
Scarce knowing whence his wounds have come;—
One other charge, Imperial Mumm,
  And over goes a batch!

Now from Regalia's lengthy nines,
Rolls up the smoke in circling lines,
And half concealing, half defines
  Full many staggering forms;
And, badly wounded in the neck,
With naught their dying falls to check,
The Brigadiers go down in wreck,
  As ships go down in storms.

When brightly beams the morning sun,
And Peace, by doughty vict'ry won,
Once more the Nation rests upon,
  Like sunlight on the grass;

Columbia, through her happy tears,
Shall thank her gallant Brigadiers,
And then go on, for years and years,
To tax — the broken glass.

THE EDITOR'S WOOING.

WE love thee, Ann Maria Smith,
  And in thy condescension,
We see a future full of joys
  Too numerous to mention.

There 's Cupid's arrow in thy glance,
  That by thy love's coercion
Has reach'd our melting heart of hearts,
  And ask'd for one insertion.

With joy we feel the blissful smart,
  And ere our passion ranges,
We freely place thy love upon
  The list of our exchanges.

There 's music in thy lowest tone,
  And silver in thy laughter;
And truth — but we will give the full
  Particulars hereafter.

Oh! we could tell thee of our plans
  All obstacles to scatter;
But we are full just now, and have
  A press of other matter.

Then let us marry, Queen of Smiths,
  Without more hesitation ;
The very thought doth give our blood
  A larger circulation !

THE POETRY OF LIFE.

THAT side of life the sun is constant to,
  Forever ripening newer buds of pleasure,
Is but a prelude to a nobler song,
  Tuned to a rambling, dithyrambic measure.

The life of childhood 's a melodious blank —
  Though nothing unsubstantial could be sweeter —
And 't is the mother's poetry revised,
  When first she trains her darling's feet to meet her.

That side of life First Love is constant to,
  With wings of hope the fever'd spirit fanning,
Gives one rhymed lesson to the Maid and Youth,
  While each the other's glowing lines is scanning.

But Sorrow, earliest, bids the Poem rise,
  And grow in strength, as Pleasure's band disperses ;
The strain sublimest is the voice of pain,
  The Poetry of Life is its Re-verses !

STICKING TO HIM.

THE mother saw her only one
  Before the parson stand,
To seal another love than hers
  With willing heart and hand;
And down her wrinkled cheek there roll'd
  A fond, regretful tear;
For, though she gain'd a son-in-law,
  She lost a daughter dear.

That daughter mark'd the sign of grief, —
  And turn'd a paler hue,
As back to childhood's helpless years
  Her thoughts reminded flew, —
And, bending from her husband's side,
  She kiss'd the hand that e'en
Had gently minister'd to her
  In all the years between.

"Dear mother, do not weep," she said;
  "Though going far away,
In two short months we both return
  To be your double stay;
And if your thoughtless daughter fails
  In duty to be done,

Look up, dear mother, for the help
  That 's stronger from a son!"

Then smiled the mother on her child,
  Such loving words to hear,
And press'd upon her glowing cheek
  The sequel of the tear;
And, raising high her trembling hands,
  When plighted was the troth,
She whisper'd, though with quiv'ring lips,
  "God bless ye, darlings, both!"

A moment did she disappear,
  And then return'd again
With something hid behind her back
  And dragg'd along amain.
Then fix'd her idolizing eyes
  Upon the youthful pair,
Where, silent in a sweet surprise,
  They stood to meet her there.

"'T is little I can spare," she said,
  "For scanty is my store;
But here accept a bridal gift
  Before ye leave my door.
Though o'er-familiar to the sight,
  And homely, it may be,
It ever nurtured peace between
  My good old man and me.

"Then take it, daughter, at the start
  Of this, thy married life,

And give thy promise as a bride
  To use it as a wife;
Nor ever in thy darkest hour
  A friend more potent crave;
For 't is the very broomstick, girl,
  That made thy sire behave!"

DISENCHANTED.

ALL hail'd her a parlor Calypso,
The Siren Supreme of the throng,
Who dazzled with jewels and satins,
And woo'd as they floated along.

Her locks were like night in the tropics,
Her brow shamed the lily in white ;
Her eyes were two oceans of darkness
Reflecting two oceans of light.

Her lips were the coralline portals,
The shrine of a heaven of bliss,
That e'en might entice the immortals
To turn, and be lost in a kiss.

Her garment, in folds dropping lustre
Trail'd softly in ripple and curl,
Seem'd wrought from the wave of a water
Whose azure had melted a pearl.

One hand reap'd a harvest of ringlets,
The other ruled grace at her side ;
Her form was the form of a maiden,
In crown of full womanly pride.

I knew her — had known her from childhood ;
  Yet, such is the magical spell
Of Beauty enthroned o'er her subjects,
  I dared not salute Anabel.

But Thought spurns the bonds of the human,
  And e'en as I gazed at her there,
I dream'd of a day in the future,
  Of all my young days the most fair.

For, had she not wept at our parting ?
  And had she not blush'd when we met ?
I saw my white rose on her bosom,
  And knew that she could not forget.

'Mid dancing, and gay conversation,
  And planning of new loves around,
I stood there alone with my idol,
  Like Silence ghost-brooding in sound.

What though she smiled others to Heaven
  With lips that were zephyr'd with mirth,
When mine was the droop of the lashes
  That gave me my heaven on earth !

At last, when the voice of a singer
  Came sweet through the tapestried door,
Her courtiers took leave of their Empress,
  And swept o'er the velveted floor.

They left her — she would not go with them,
  And I, in the red curtain's glow,

Was thrill'd with such loving emotions
  As none but a lover can know.

I thought, in my joy, to surprise her;
  But paused, as I lifted a fold,
And saw her draw forth from her bosom
  A quaint little casket of gold.

The horrors of jealousy smote me —
  The face of a Rival! thought I;
But scarce had a minute flown over,
  When more was exposed to my eye.

The casket was stealthily opened,
  A hand shed its whiteness within,
And forth from its secret recesses
  Brought something of silver, or tin.

She dipp'd it low down in the casket —
  Glanced anxiously round, as in fear,
Then parted her lips in a moment,
  And plunged it between with a smear!

I saw it, recoiling in horror!
  One glimpse of the scene was enough;
The thing in her mouth was a "Dipper,"
  The casket, a casket of snuff.

O, what was the glow of her blushes,
  O, what was the glance of her eye?
The flush of a deep dissipation,
  The fire that but sparkled to die!

My vision of loveliness faded,
  My passion was turn'd to disdain ;
I crept from the place like a shadow,
  And never shall enter again.

THE NEUTRAL BRITISH GENTLEMAN.

INCRUSTED in his island home that lies beyond the sea,
Behold the great original and genuine 'T IS HE;
A paunchy, fuming Son of Beef, with double weight of chin,
And eyes that were benevolent, — but for their singular tendency to turn green whenever it is remarked that his irrepressible American cousins have made another Treaty with China ahead of him, — and taken Albion in.
This Neutral British Gentleman, one of the modern time.

With William, Duke of Normandy, his ancestors, he boasts,
Came over from the shores of France to whip the Saxon hosts;
And this he makes a source of pride; but wherefore there should be
Such credit to an Englishman — in the fact that he is descended from a nation which England is forever pretending to regard as slightly her inferior in everything, and particularly behind her in military and naval affairs — we really cannot see.
This Neutral British Gentleman, one of the modern time.

He deals in Christianity, Episcopalian brand,
And sends his missionaries forth to bully heathen land;
Just mention "Slavery" to him, and with a pious sigh
He 'll say it 's 'orrid, scandalous — although he 's ready to fight for the Cotton raised by slaves, and forgets how he butchered the Chinese to make them take Opium, and blew the Sepoys from the guns because the poor devils refused to be enslaved by the East India Company — or his phi-lan-thro-py.
This Neutral British Gentleman, one of the modern time.

He yields to Brother Jonathan a love that passeth show, —
"We 're Hanglo-Saxons, both of us, and carn't be foes, you know."
But as a Christian Englishman, he cannot, cannot hide
His horror of the spectacle — of four millions of black beings boldly held in bondage by a nation professing the largest liberty in the world, though in case of an anti-slavery crusade the interests of his Manchester factors would imperatively forbid him to — take part on either side.
This Neutral British Gentleman, one of the modern time.

Now seeing the said Jonathan by base rebellion stirr'd,
And battling with pro-slavery, it might be thence inferr'd
That British sympathy, at last, would spur him on to strife;

But, strange to say, this sympathy — is labelled "NEUTRALITY," and consigned to any rebel port not too closely blockaded to permit English vessels, loaded with munitions, to slip in. And when you ask Mr. Bull what he means by this inconsistent conduct, he becomes virtuously indignant, rolls up his eyes, and says: "I carn't endure to see brothers murdering each other and keeping me out of my cotton — I carn't, upon my life!"

This Neutral British Gentleman, one of the modern time.

Supposing Mr. Bull should die, the question might arise:

Will he be wanted down below, or wafted to the skies?

Allowing that he had his choice, it really seems to me

The moral British Gentleman — would choose a front seat with his Infernal Majesty; since Milton, in his blank verse correspondence with old *Times*, more than once hinted the possibility of Nick's rebellion against Heaven succeeding; and as the Lower Secessia cottoned to England through numerous Hanoverian reigns, such a choice on the part of the philanthropical Britisher would be simply another specimen — of his NEUTRAL-I-TY!

This Neutral British Gentleman, one of the modern time.

A COMPROMISE.

YOU call it Cant, O Strong of Mind!
  When, heeding human nature's plan,
We doubt if you are fit for all
  That is the more becoming Man.

If only shallow cant it be,
  True wisdom's honest ear to vex,
By something more than scolding prove
  The manly genius of your sex.

When Woman, by her science, shows
  The subtle lightning how to write;
When Woman, by her brain, shall teach
  A nation's army how to fight;

When Woman's mastery of State,
  Shall, like another Wheaton's, rule;
When Woman a Colenso comes,
  To lead a higher churchman's school;

When Woman, by mechanic-skill,
  A second Reaper shall invent;
When Woman, by her pen, shall match
  A Story, Blackstone, or a Kent;—

She, in the workshop, court of law,
  The field of arms, or field of grain,
The Council of the Church, or State,
  May equal place with Man attain.

And 'till she thus a fitness proves
  For Rights for which her sex may pant,
We, Men, remain but those who Can,
  And she and hers the ones who Can't!

Yet if for her there needs must be
  Some chance above herself to rise,
Without distraction to the world
  There still may be a compromise:

Let Woman not for voting stir,
  But learn the barber's trade instead;
So shall the Poll be brought to her,
  To razor o'er her husband's head.

ILLITERARIA.

SOUTHWESTERN SKETCHES.

BY "THE ARKANSAW NIGHTINGALE."

THE BEWITCHED TERRIER.

SAM JOHNSON was a cullud man
  Who lived down in Judee ;
He owned a rat tan tarrier
  That stood 'bout one foot three ;
And the way that critter chaw'd up rats
  Was gorjus for to see.

One day this dorg was slumberin'
  Behind the kitchen stove,
When suddenly a wicked flea —
  An ugly little cove —
Began upon his faithful back
  With many jumps to rove.

Then up arose that tarrier,
  With frenzy in his eye,
And waitin' only long enough
  To make a touchin' cry,
Commenced to twist his head around,
  Most wonderfully spry.

But all in vain ; his shape was sich,
  So awful short and fat —
That though he doubled up hisself,
  And strain'd hisself at that,
His mouth was half an inch away
  From where the varmint sat.

The dorg sat up an awful yowl
  And twisted like an eel,
Emitting cries of misery
  At ev'ry nip he 'd feel,
And tumblin' down and jumpin' up,
  And turnin' like a wheel.

But still that most owdacious flea
  Kept up a constant chaw
Just where he could n't be scratch'd out
  By any reach of paw,
But always half an inch beyond
  His wictim's snappin' jaw.

Sam Johnson heard the noise, and came
  To save his animile ;
But when he see the crittur spin —
  A barkin' all the while —
He dreaded hiderfobia,
  And then began to rile.

"The pup is mad enough," says he,
  And luggin' in his axe,
He gev the wretched tarrier
  A pair of awful cracks,

That stretch'd him out upon the floor,
   As dead as carpet-tacks.

Take warnin' by this tarrier
   And keep.this p'int in view :
The wicked Flea, when no men but
   The reachers him pursue,
Is bold as any lion, just
   To prove the Scripters true.

TUSCALOOSA SAM.

THERE was a man in Arkansaw
 As let his passions rise,
And not unfrequently pick'd out
 Some other varmint's eyes.

His name was Tuscaloosa Sam,
 And often he would say,
" There 's not a cuss in Arkansaw
 I can't whip any day."

One morn, a stranger passin' by,
 Heard Sammy talkin' so,
When down he scrambled from his hoss,
 And off his coat did go.

He sorter kinder shut one eye,
 And spit into his hand,
And put his ugly head one side,
 And twitch'd his trousers' band.

" My boy," says he, " it 's my belief,
 Whomever you may be,
That I kin make you screech, and smell
 Pertikler agony."

" I 'm thar," says Tuscaloosa Sam,
  And chuck'd his hat away ;
" I 'm thar," says he, and button'd up
  As far as buttons may.

They clinch'd like two rampageous bears,
  And then went down a bit ;
They swore a stream of six-inch oaths
  And fit, and fit, and fit.

When Sam would try to work away,
  And on his pegs to git,
The stranger 'd pull him back ; and so,
  They fit, and fit, and fit !

Then like a pair of lobsters, both
  Upon the ground were knit,
And yet the varmints used their teeth,
  And fit, and fit, and fit ! !

The sun of noon was high above,
  And hot enough to split,
But only riled the fellers more,
  That fit, and fit, and fit ! ! !

The stranger snapp'd at Sammy's nose,
  And shorten'd it a bit ;
And then they both swore awful hard,
  And fit, and fit, and fit ! ! ! !

The mud it flew, the sky grew dark,
  And all the litenins lit ;

But still them critters roll'd about
  And fit, and fit, and fit ! ! ! ! !

First Sam on top, then t'other chap ;
  When one would make a hit,
The other 'd smell the grass ; and so,
  They fit, and fit, and fit ! ! ! ! ! !

The night came on, the stars shone out
  As bright as wimmen's wit ;
And still them fellers swore and gouged,
  And fit, and fit, and fit ! ! ! ! ! ! !

The neighbors heard the noise they made,
  And thought an earthquake lit ;
Yet all the while 't was him and Sam
  As fit, and fit, and fit ! ! ! ! ! ! ! !

For miles around the noise was heard ;
  Folks could n't sleep a bit,
Because them two rantank'rous chaps
  Still fit, and fit, and fit ! ! ! ! ! ! ! ! !

But jist at cock-crow, suddently,
  There came an awful pause,
And I and my old man run out
  To ascertain the cause.

The sun was rising in the yeast,
  And lit the hull concern ;
But not a sign of either chap
  Was found at any turn.

Yet, in the region where they fit,
  We found, to our surprise,
One pint of buttons, two big knives,
  Some whiskers, and four eyes !

'LIGE SIMMONS'S DOG.

'LIGE SIMMONS is as 'cute a chap
  As ever you did see,
And when the feller says a thing,
  It 's sure as it can be.

He owns a dog — and sich a brute
  For gettin' round a chap,
I never see in all my life,
  You 'd better bet your cap.

Now 'Lige is proud of this here dog,
  And says the critter 'll whip
As many wild-cats in an hour
  As go to load a ship.

" But law," says 'Lige, " that animile
  Is awful in a row,
And other pups 'longside of him
  An't no account, nohow."

In fact, one day, I saw the same
  Contemporaneous pup
Pitch into a Newfoundlander
  And chaw him slightly up.

He 's such a plaguy little cuss,
  You 'd laugh to see him come ;
But when there 's chawin' up to do
  I tell you, boss, he 's some !

One day, a pedler came to town
  With ginger-beer and things,
And patent clocks, and pious books,
  And fancy finger-rings.

And underneath his cart was tied
  A bull-dog of the kind
That tears your musn't-mention-'ems,
  In angry frame of mind.

Now 'Lige's dog was smellin' round,
  And when he see this here,
He cock'd his eye in agony,
  And acted awful queer.

The bull-dog gin a rousin' shout,
  As 'Lige's dog went by,
And gev him such a sassy nip
  That fur began to fly.

Then 'Lige's dog unfurl'd his tail
  And gev the wound a lick,
And then pitch'd into that ere dog
  A way that *was n't* sick.

The critters had it nip and tuck,
  And made such awful noise,

That 'Lige himself came up to see,
With all the other boys.

The pedler see him, and says he,
Like one to fits inured :
" I 'm sorry, strannger ; but I hope
Your yaller dog 's insured."

I tell you, boys, 't was fun to see
The grin that 'Lige put on,
As in his cheek he put a chaw
And wink'd his eye at one.

" O, let the varmints fit," says 'Lige,
" My pup is awful thin,
And this here row will make him look
Jist like himself ag'in."

And all this while the fit went on,
With such a mess of dust
We could n't tell the upper dog,
If all our eyes should bust.

'T was yell and yowl, and shout and growl,
And stompin' awful hard,
And sometimes ther 'd a tail stick out
From where the dust was bar'd.

Byme-by the noise began to die,
And as it fainter grew,
The dust began to settle down,
And you could just see through.

At last it clear'd away entire,
  But all that we could see
Was 'Lige's dog a squattin' down
  Beneath the axletree.

"Law!" says the pedler, lookin' blue,
  "What 's happened to *my* pup?"
Says 'Lige: "It 's my opinion, boss,
  My pup has eat him up."

"But where 's the chain I tied him with?"
  The pedler loud did call.
And would you b'lieve me — 'Lige's dog
  Had swallow'd chain and all!

One end was hangin' from his mouth
  And gev him such a cough,
We had to fetch a chisel out
  And cut some inches off.

The pedler dropp'd a tear, and then
  Says he to 'Lige, says he:
"I 'd like to buy that yaller pup
  And take him home with me."

But "no," says 'Lige, with proud disdain,
  And sot down on a log,
"That pup is plural now, you know —
  A dog within a dog."

"He 's twice as strong to fit," says 'Lige;
  "For if he 's kill'd outside,

I 'll turn the critter inside out,
  And let *your* critter slide."

" Well," says the pedler, with a sigh,
  " The pup 's a trump, I think ;
But let us change the subject now ;
  Say, strannger ! — do you drink ? "

THE PHANTOM GOAT.

THERE wuz a rather oldish chap
  That lived in Tennessee;
A parson of the Methodists,
  With mighty beard, was he.

It wuz a mighty beard, you bet,
  That wagg'd upon his breast,
And when the good old cuss would talk
  It work'd like all possest.

This good old cuss he had a goat
  He 'd kept for many years,
And how they loved each other well
  Would move a pump to tears.

The goat would run to meet the cuss
  When air he heard his tread,
And then the parson he would stoop
  To scratch poor Billy's head.

But when the smashin' war broke out
  Purvisions got so scurce,
The parson found it would n't pay
  An idle beast to nurse;

And so, one day the good old cuss
His ancient friend did fell;
And having skinn'd and salted him
Did live on him a spell.

But O, it went agin the grain
This cruel deed to do,
And, having eaten up the goat,
The parson wept boo-hoo.

The more he thought on that air deed
The more he did repent,
And bitterly he cuss'd the axe
With which he let it went.

It prey'd so awful on his mind,
That even in his sleep
He pluck'd his beard, and kick'd about,
And in a dream did weep.

One moonlight night he woke him up,
And, rising on his cot,
Beheld, almost beside his bed,
A vision of his goat!

He nods his head, the goat nods his;
The parson gives a groan
And settles down amongst the quilts
A shakin' to the bone.

Next night the same, and so the next;
The moonlight still reveals

The features of a fantom goat,
  But lately used at meals.

The good old cuss, he bore the thing
  Till conquer'd by his fright,
And then he went and got a friend
  To stay with him a night.

'T was half past ten when this here friend
  Was call'd unto the cot,
And lo! the parson showed to him
  The spectre of the goat.

The friend he look'd with eager eyes
  To see what he could see,
And then he bust into a larf,
  A reg'lar he! he! he!

Then gravely said the good old cuss,
  "Why larf you so, my friend?
The reason of your levity
  I cannot comprehend."

"Because, old man," the friend return'd,
  "That goat 's no ghostly elf,
But your own head and beard within
  The mirror on the shelf!"

And so it was! The good old cuss,
  Inspired with fear and awe,
Was all but scared to death when he
  His own reflection saw.

For when the light fell on the glass,
And he sat on his cot,
The former caught his head and beard
And made of them a goat!

Be careful you who wear your beards
Half-way up to your eyes,
Or in some looking-glass you 'll see
A fantom goat likewise!

PAUDEEN.

BY RAPHAEL ST. JOHN.

[A volunteer commentator writes a note introducing the extraordinary verses given below, lauding them in a most extravagant and outrageous manner. To quote his own inflated terms: "The author of the following exquisitely pathetic — I may almost say holy — illustration of the true Sublimity ever to be found even in the most dissipated type of human depravity, bears the hitherto obscure name of Raphael St. John, and is as refined as he is beautiful. Of unknown age and pedigree; with wavy golden locks floating from his white temples nearly to the ground, and great, spiritual hazel eyes, directed meekly upwards through the long, silken lashes, half the time; with features daintily true to the most delicate ideal of an outward bespeaking an inward Purity, and a lithe, willowy form subserving the most spiritualized model of childish Grace, Raphael St. John at once impresses the beholder with an idea of Apostolic power combined with the most subtle delicacy." After some further raving enthusiasticalities of personal description, celebrating the unassuming piety and Christian cleanliness of "Raphael St. John's tenderly analytical soul," our excited commentator goes on to say that "in 'Paudeen,' with its wonderfully faithful domestic lights and shades of American life and honest human nature, we have nothing less than the first, fresh, full, melodious note of the long-expected New American Literature! As though his own marvellous instinct divined as much, it has inspired the unwitting sweet singer to assimilate the wondrous prosody of his precious Lyric for Humanity to the national air of '*The Star-Spangled Banner!*' What a perfect fitness is here! How gracefully becoming is it that the first piece of distinctively American writing ever produced by American genius should, by the merest apparent accident, be susceptible of popular vocalization to a tune which embalms the most glorious of national memories!"]

SINFUL SAM is my name, I confess, to my shame,
And tears for the same are both frequent and briny;
But I 'll put up the soap that there 's always a hope
For crimes that are scarlet, to make them wash shiny —

Or, at least, so it said
In a Book I heard read,
Before my old mother took cold and went dead.
Though the name of that Volume recurs not to me,
'T was a something, you bet, that began with a B.

Not myself, though, I mean, as it 's plain to be seen,
But Contrite Paudeen, who was scarlet as blazes;
At the close of the day in his shanty he lay,
From manifold drinks of the liquid which crazes;
And his language was such,
And repeated so much,
That — although it was anything rather than Dutch —
To describe its chief term I can only make free
With a hint that it open'd and ended with D.

Looking up with a stare, as I sat on a chair,
He tore out his hair, which in color was florid;
And I saw the hot drop here and there on the top
Of what was his scanty two inches of forehead.
"Bloody blazes!" says he,
"Is it Snakes that I see?
Keep 'em off! or, Old Woman, I 'll wring your" — but P.,
When his good wife addressing, would yearn, now and then,
To playfully wring what began with an N.

To console him I tried, and his vision denied,
While proving, beside, that he only was dreaming;
"Put your head on my breast, and compose you to rest,
Old pal!" I remark'd, "and let up with your screaming."

Then he gave but one yell,
Though his eyes roll'd a spell;
Like a wearisome child on my bosom he fell —
"Hold me up! you infernal old" — ah, well-a-day,
'T was his pet name for me, and began with an A.

"Are you Dying?" I said, as his dear bullet-head
Kept sinking, like lead, from my shoulder so trembling;
"You old sardine, reply! Is it all in your eye?
O say, if you can, that you are but dissembling!"
"I am caving," moan'd he,
With a clutch at my knee,
"And it 's roasting red-hot that I quickly shall be.
Who will then be a father to poor little 'Jeff,'
But yourself, you confounded" — first letter an F.

"Care for 'Jeff,' — the bull-pup, — that you 've always back'd up
With stamps, though no sup was for wife or for babies?
That I will, my old pal; have the best care he shall —
Or may I go mad with his consequent rabies!"
Thus I made him reply,
And Paudeen winked his eye:
"I 'm content — True-American-like let me die!"
With a smile on his lip on his pillow he fell —
"Sick him, — Jeff! — give him" — something that ended in l.

Sinful Sam is my name, I confess, to my shame,
And tears for the same are both frequent and briny;
But I 'll put up the soap that there 's always a hope
For crimes that are scarlet, to make them wash shiny.

Or a Book says, at least,
Something kind, Mr. Priest,
For the merciful man who is good to his beast.
Though the name of the Volume recurs not to me,
'T is a something, you bet, that begins with a B.*

* While conceding to the above lyric all the credit for delicacy and reverence due to its artless substitution of initials for objectionable full words, and acknowledging that the curious coincidence of its rhythm with that of a popular national air *does* go very far indeed to stamp it as intrinsically American, the judicious critic must still question whether an expiring unmitigated ruffian's mortuary tenderness for his fighting dog, occurring simultaneously with his entire forgetfulness of his ill-used wife and possible children, is, even in the interest of a new native literature, the full justification that a rigorous theologian might think necessary for such phrasing of things sacred as can be sung to the air of "The Star-Spangled Banner."

DE GREAT HALLELUGERUM.

BY A "CONTRABAND" REFUGEE. (1863.)

MY mars'r 's gwine away to fight
With Mars'r Linkum's horde,
An' now dis chile 's at libaty
To dance an' bress de Lord.
Dar 's no more swearin' round de house
When missus cut up bad;
Dar 's no more kickin' niggers' shins,
And, darfor', I is glad.

When mars'r take his horse to go,
He kindly say to me:
"I hab such confidence in you,
I leab you all, you see;
Of all de niggers round de place,
I trust to you alone."
By golly! dat 's what mars'r say
To eb'ry nig he own!

"Now if dem Bobumlitionists
Should kill me dead," says he,
"I hab instruct your missus kind
To set you niggers free."

But mars'r say dat bery same
  Wheneber he get sick,
And bresséd Jesus wrastle him
  To make him holy quick.

" Dem Yankees, dam um all," says he,
  " Am comin' down to steal
You niggers, and to sell you then
  For Cuba cochineal.
De Suvern chiverly," says he,
  " Am fightin' jist fo' you."
Now mars'r swearum when he lie,
  And, darfor', dat won't do!

Den mars'r trot away to war
  With 'Dolphus by his side, —
A poor cream-color'd, common dark
  Dat is n't worf his hide.
He leab me and de other nigs
  To clar the place alone,
With nuffin' but to play and shake
  De fiddle and de bone.

I hab a talk with Uncle Pete,
  De old plantation hand,
And, though he am intelligums,
  Dis chile can understand.
He say de Hallelugerum
  For cullud folks hab cum,
And dat de bresséd Lord hab heard
  And beat his thunder-drum.

He say dat Northern buckra man
  Hab sent his gun an' ship
To make de rebel chiverly
  Give up his nigger whip;
He say dat now 's de darkey's time
  To break de bonds of sin,
And take his chil'en an' his wife
  To whar de tide comes in.

He say dat in de Norf, up dar,
  Whar Mars'r Greeley dwell,
De white folks make de brack folks work,
  But treat them bery well;
He says dey pay them for de work
  Dey 's smart enuff to do,
And nebber sells them furder Souf
  When sheriff put um screw.

I hab a wife an' chil'en dear,
  And mars'r say to me,
He nebber sell them while he live, —
  He 'd rather set them free;
But dar 's de mortgage on de house,
  If dat should hab to fall,
Ole Uncle Pete hab told me dat
  He 'd hab to sell us all.

I lub de ole plantation well,
  And missus she is kind;
But den dis chile 's inclined to try
  Another home to find.

Now mars'r gwine away to war,
 And give me such a chance,
I 'll bress de Lord for libaty,
 And hab a Juba dance.

De Hallelugerum am cum
 With glory in his eye,
And all de niggers in de Souf
 Am fit to mount de sky.
My wife an' chil'en hab de spoons
 Dat 's owned by — (here a cough) —
I hab de sugar-tongs myself,
 And, darfor', I is off.

THE UNIVERSAL EXILE'S LAMENT.

ATTIND to me, mother, while loud I 'm complaining,
And bend your swate eyes more complately to hear;
For weakness of voice is just all I am gaining,
Locked up in a jail, with no comrade to cheer.
Ye 'll say it 's from jail that I 'm always a-writing,
Ah, true is the story — *pieta di me!*
And now, as before, what has caused my indicting
Is just my insisting, that
Man MUST be free!

But twinty years old was my age as I reckon,
When one of my friends had his landlord to pay;
And quick we agreed, o'er a bottle of whiskey,
To settle the rint with shillalies in play.
It 's somebody's head that I crack'd in a jiffy, —
My own sunny France, I was striking for thee! —
And straight to a prison *les tyrans* convey'd me,
Despite my protesting that
Man MUST be free!

I served like a baste through my period penal,
Wi' a' the composure auld Reekie inspires;
And spake to the judge in his altitude venal,
As one in whose bosom were liberty's fires.

Then home I repair'd ; but, before I got thither,
A bit of a mob made me join in their glee ;
It 's government houses we burn'd, and some people,
To prove we were drunk, and that
Man MUST be free !

Myself did they take, with some dozens of others,
And gave us a trial for trayson indade ;
And sintinced us all, right in sight of our mothers,
To cross the wide ocean with fetters and spade.
Not *ein hohes wort* was in all of their charges :
But stern was the Justice, and, " Pris'ner," says he,
"How came you to join in this burning and stealing ? "
" To show," says I, boldly, " that
Man MUST be free ! "

When safely arrived at the scene of our labors,
I found the Commandant quite gintly inclined ;
He singled me out from the midst of my neighbors,
And softly I gave him a piece of my mind :
" I 'm sickly," says I, " and have nade of indulgence,
Nor will I abuse it if given to me."
He trusted my word and indulged me, *per Baccho*,
And soon I escaped, because
Man MUST be free !

Then straight to this country I fled for protection,
And was n't I hailed as a patriot born ?
They asked me to stand for a local election, —
But such a small offer I treated with scorn.
And soon did I join, with an energy aygur,
Some gintleman proud as it 's aisy to be,

Who went into fighting for keeping the naygur,
  And showing, *per Dio*, that
          Man MUST be free!

Bad luck to it all! 't was a bating they gave us;
  And *Allah il Allah!* was all I could say;
From starving down South there was nothing to save us,
  And I was not slow about coming away:
It 's not for a pardon I 'd ask of the rulers,
  Nor yet would I seek from the country to flee;
For what could they do in a real republic
  To one who said only that
          Man MUST be free!

Not troubled at all in me mind for the morrow,
  I turn'd my attintion to matters of State;
And so, having fail'd, to my infinite sorrow,
  In fighting the nation, took comfort of fate.
'Twas right in the midst of advising the rulers
  Just how they should act to the South, and to me, —
When "*Credat Judæus!*" they say; and I 'm taken
  To jail, though explaining that
          Man MUST be free!

Sure, mother, but Liberty 's all a delusion,
  And Italy, Hungary, Poland, and I,
Can only be kept in eternal confusion
  By hoping for landlords and despots to die.
So, here let me say, in the musical tongue of
  My own native Venice — *Venite per me!*
It 's most of me time that I 'm spending in prison,
  And all from insisting that
          Man MUST be free!

THE IRISH RECRUIT.

TWO Irishmen out of employ,
  And out at the elbows as aisily,
Adrift in a grocery-store
  Were smoking and taking it lazily.
The one was a broth of a boy,
  Whose cheek-bones turn'd out and turn'd in again,
His name it was Paddy O'Toole —
  The other was Misther McFinnigan.

"I think of enlistin'," says Pat,
  "Because do you see what o'clock it is;
There 's nothin' adoin' at all
  But drinkin' at Mrs. O'Docharty's.
It 's not until after the war
  That business times will begin again,
And fightin' 's the duty of all" —
  "You 're right, sir," says Misther McFinnigan.

"Bad luck to the rebels, I say,
  For kickin' up all of this bobbery,
They call themselves gintlemen, too,
  While practisin' murder and robbery;
Now if it 's gintale for to steal,
  And take all your creditors in again,

I 'm glad I 'm no gintleman born" —
  "You 're right, sir," says Misther McFinnigan.

"The spalpeens make bould to remark
  Their chivalry could n't be ruled by us;
And by the same token I think
  They 're never too smart to be fool'd by us.
Now if it 's the naygurs they mane
  Be chivalry, then it 's a sin again
To fight for a cause that is black" —
  "You 're right, sir," says Misther McFinnigan.

"A naygur 's a man, ye may say,
  And aiqual to all other Southerners;
But chivalry 's made him a brute,
  And so he 's a monkey to Northerners;
Sure, look at the poor cratur's heels,
  And look at his singular shin again;
It 's not for such gintlemen fight" —
  "You 're right, sir," says Misther McFinnigan.

"The naygur States wanted a row,
  And now, be me sowl, but they 've got in it!
They 've chosen a bed that is hard,
  However they shtrive for to cotton it.
I 'm thinkin', when winter comes on
  They 'll all be inclined to come in again;
But then we must bate them at first" —
  "You 're right, sir," says Misther McFinnigan.

"Och hone! but it 's hard that a swate
  Good-lookin' young chap like myself, indade,

Should loose his ten shillin's a day
  Because of the throuble the South has made:
But that 's just the raison, ye see,
  Why I should help Union to win again.
It 's that will bring wages once more" —
  "You 're right, sir," says Misther McFinnigan.

"Joost mind what ould England's about,
  A-sendin' her throops into Canaday;
And all her ould ships on the coast
  Are ripe for some threachery any day.
Now if she should mix in the war —
  Be jabers! it makes me head spin again!
Ould Ireland would have such a chance!" —
  "You 're right, sir," says Misther McFinnigan.

"You talk about Irishmen, now,
  Enlistin' by thousands from loyalty;
But wait till the Phœnix Brigade
  Is called to put down British Royalty!
It 's then with the Stars and the Stripes
  All Irishmen here would go in again,
To strike for the Shamrock and Harp!"
  "You 're right, sir," says Misther McFinnigan.

"Och, murther! me blood 's in a blaze,
  To think of bould Corcoran leading us,
Right into the camp of the bastes
  Whose leeches so long have been bleeding us!
The Stars and the Stripes here at home
  To Canada's wall we would pin again,
And would n't we raise them in Cork?" —
  "You 're right, sir," says Misther McFinnigan.

"And down at the South, do ye mind,
 There 's plinty of Irishmen mustering,
Deluded to fight for the wrong
 By rebel misstatements and blustering;
But once let ould England, their foe,
 To fight with the Union begin again,
And, sure, they 'd desert to a man!" —
 "You 're right, sir," says Misther McFinnigan.

"There 's niver an Irishmen born,
 From Maine to the end of Secessiondom,
But longs for a time and a chance
 To fight for this country in Hessian-dom;
And so, if ould England should thry
 With treacherous friendship to sin again,
They 'll all be on one side at once" —
 "You 're right, sir," says Misther McFinnigan.

"We 've brothers in Canada, too —
 (And did n't the Prince have a taste of them?) —
To say that to Ireland they 're true
 Is certainly saying the laste of them.
If, bearing our flag at our head,
 We rose Ireland's freedom to win again,
They 'd murther John Bull in the rear!" —
 "You 're right, sir," says Misther McFinnigan.

"Hurroo! for the Union, me boy!
 And divil take all who would bother it,
Secession 's a naygur so black
 The divil himself ought to father it;
Hurroo! for the bould 69th,
 That 's prisintly bound to go in again;

It's Corcoran's rescue they 're at" —
  "You 're right, sir," says Misther McFinnigan.

" I 'm off right away to enlist,
  And sure won't the bounty be handy-O!
To kape me respectably dress'd
  And furnish me dudheens and brandy-O!
I 'm thinkin', me excellent fri'nd,
  Ye 're eying that bottle of gin again;
You would n't mind thryin' a drop" —
  "You 're right, sir," says Misther McFinnigan.

WIDOW MACSHANE.

NEAR ould Skibbereen, in the gim of the owshun,
The spaker was born, in a quare-lookin' place,
Where pigs and a cow were in full locomowshun,
And six other childers were shlapein' in pace.

I cannot say mooch for me father's exthraction,
Because, do ye see, he was born in the bogs;
But as for me mother, be double transaction,
She loved the ould chap and the rest of the hogs.

'T was joost as I enter'd this wurruld of slaughter,
Me father looked up from his sate be the wall;
Says he, "Me swate Bridget, pray how is our daughter?"
Says she, "Ye ould fool, it's no daughter at all!"

"Och murther an' turf!" he exclaim'd in a passion,
And struck wid his fisht on the top of his knee;
His ancient dudheen in the corner went smashin',
And all on account of perverseness in me!

"Ye red-lookin' thafe!" says the gintle ould sinner,
Adthressing his illigant languidge to me,
"'T is a nice-lookin' mout that ye have for a dinner!"
But I was too spacheless his maneing to see.

"I swore it," says he, "be the sowl of Saint Payther,
  A nate little daughter should be me next son ;
But since ye have chosen a maskelin nayther,
  I 'm bound to disown ye, as sure as a gun !

"I hope ye will mate wid the price of transgression,
  Whativer the craytures ye tarry among ;
And mark me, me lad ! 't is me private impression
  Ye niver will die 'till the day ye are hoong !"

"Be quiet, me angil," says Bridget, me mother,
  "'T is aisy to talk when the mischief is done ;
Who knows but some day ye may want for a brother !
  And thin ye 'll be glad that yere girl is a son !"

(The wimmin are prophets, wheriver ye find 'em ;
  For many 's the time I have help'd me poor dad
To see the door latchet directly behind him,
  And sometimes to walk — whin the whiskey was bad !)

The way I was bate from the night till the mornin',
  And thin from the mornin' again till to bed,
Should be unto aich sivinth son a sad warnin'
  Against gettin' born till his father is dead.

But batins are said to agree wid some people ;
  And sure they were blessin's that caused me to grow
Until I was almost as tall as a staple, —
  And only fell short be an acre or so.

Wan mornin' whin I was ingaged in the gardin',
  Me father came up wid his pipe in his mout ;

And "Barney," says he, "I must crave for yere pardin ;
  But tell me, ye spalpeen, what *are* ye about?"

"'T is hoein' the praties," says I, wid affection ;
  Says he, "'T is a mighty big mout ye have got ;
And sure ye 'd devour, widout frind or connection,
  As mooch as would grow on a tin acre lot.

"Me farrum, ye know, is not quite so extinsive,
  And, though I 'm as fond of ye now as me breath,
I 'm fear'd, as yere appetite 's so comprehinsive,
  Ye 'll stay here to ate till yere starvin' to death."

"Yer servant," said I, like a dignified crayture,
  "And hoe for yersilf in the future," says I ;
"For since I am sthrong as yersilf in me stature,
  I don't mind remarkin' to ye that ye lie !

"The wurruld invites me to walk on her bussum,
  And sthrive for a place in the council of state ;
And niver has Fortune a low-hangin' blossom,
  But I, like a bee, will extract all its shwate."

"Thin walk on the bussom, me darlin'," he groonted,
  "But mind that ye niver get down in the mout ;
Nor go to the land where an Irishman 's hoonted
  By oogly know-nothings that 's lurkin' about."

I scorn'd to reply to the spacious suggestion ;
  But put me wardrobe in the crown of me hat ;
And, kissing me mother, to aid me digestion,
  Set out on me thravels as still as a cat.

Ye mind there 's a kingdom called Donnybrook famous,
'T was there that I wint an adventure to mate;
And whin I arrived I was weary and lame as
A baste of the plough wid no legs to his fait.

Bad luck to the fortune that carried me in it!
And sure 't is the mem'ry that gives me a pain;
For scarce had I been in the tavern a minute
Whin I fell a victim to Widow MacShane!

'T was she was the landlord that thrated me dacent,
And put me to bed wid a brick in me head;
And put some more bricks in a bottle adjacent
To kape out the cowld whin me arrum was bled.

And be the same token I came for to love her,
And ask'd her to thry the high-menial line;
She called me "an in-sin-i-*va*-tin' young rover,"
And put her big mout on a fayture of mine!

Och murther an' ounds! was the divil behind me,
To blind me affection an' worry me brain?
Or was it the coorse of me father resigned me
Into the fat arrums of Widow MacShane?

And sure she had childers, the wildest young divils
That iver disgraced a respictable place;
And wan of me first matrimonial evils
Was havin' their scratches all over me face!

"Me darlin'," I said to their illigant mother,
"The childers are rayther too forward," says I;

Whin grabbin' a poker, or somethin' or other,
  She gave me a whack in the small of me thigh!

Because I complain'd of sooch singular tratement,
  She made it appear most uncommonly plain
That I was a baste, whin compared with the statement
  Of all the shwate virtues of Misther MacShane!

Och! sure sooch a life as I led wid the crayture
  Would make the most patient of madmen insane!
And often convaynient I found to my nature
  To invy the ghosht of departed MacShane!

If I did n't wear an ould shirt for a saison,
  And kape it remarkably rigid and clane,
That woman would niver be timpted to raison,
  But talk'd of the nateness of Misther MacShane!

Whiniver the night spread abroad her dark pinions,
  Thim childers would chatter like monkies in pain;
And thin I was call'd from me drame-land dominions
  To comfort the spalpeens of Misther MacShane!

If coxcombs and guardsmen made love to me woman,
  And I, in me innocence, chose to complain,
She 'd intimate sthrongly that I was inhuman,
  And mintion me contrast wid Misther MacShane!

If I took a shillin' to get me some whiskey,
  And did n't remimber to stale it again,
Be all of the Pow'rs but she 'd grow mighty frisky,
  And threaten to send me to — Misther MacShane!

I niver went out of the house in the mornin'
  Until it was night of the avening befoor;
Because she would give me a dilicate warnin'
  To manage the childers and scrub up the floor!

And whin I would vinture to spake like an aiqual,
  And tell her she acted confoundedly mane;
She 'd tell me a sthory, and tell me the saiquel!
  The life and the *death* of wan Misther MacShane!!

I lived like a baste that is kill'd be its master,
  Until I was taken wid prisince of brain;
And thin, niver lightning could thravel mooch faster
  Than I from the relic of Misther MacShane!

I came to this coonthry of freedom and progress;
  And only had been here a couple of hours,
When I was elected a mimber of Congress —
  Or daycintly ask'd to be sooch, be the Pow'rs!

But I shall go back to me gim of the owshun
  As soon as me widow is married again,
To give a free vint to me pow'rful emoshun,
  And dance on the grave of ould Misther MacShane!

THE IRISH PICKET.

I'M shtanding in the mud, Biddy,
  Wid not a spalpeen near,
And silence, spaichless as the grave,
  Is all the sound I hear.
Me gun is at a showlder arms,
  I 'm wetted to the bone,
And whin I 'm afther shpakein' out,
  I find meself alone.

This Southern climate 's quare, Biddy,
  A quare and bastely thing,
Wid Winter absint all the year,
  And Summer in the Spring.
Ye mind the hot place down below?
  And may ye niver fear
I 'd dthraw comparisons — but then
  It 's awful warrum here.

The only moon I see, Biddy,
  Is one shmall star, asthore,
And that 's fornint the very cloud
  It was behind before;
The watchfires glame along the hill
  That 's swellin' to the south,

And whin the sentry passes them
  I see his oogly mouth.

It 's dead for shlape I am, Biddy,
  And dthramein shwate I 'd be,
If them owld rebels over there
  Would only lave me free;
But when I lane against a shtump
  And shtrive to get repose,
A musket-ball be 's comin' shtraight
  To hit me spacious nose.

It 's ye I 'd like to see, Biddy,
  A shparkin' here wid me,
And then, avourneen, hear ye say,
  "Acushla — Pat — machree!"
"Och, Biddy darlint," then says I,
  Says you, "Get out of that";
Says I, "Me arrum mates your waist,"
  Says you, "Be daycent, Pat."

And how 's the pigs and ducks, Biddy?
  It 's them I think of, shure,
That look'd so innocent and shwate
  Upon the parlor flure;
I 'm shure ye 're aisy with the pig
  That 's fat as he can be,
And fade him wid the best, because
  I 'm towld he looks like me.

Whin I come home again, Biddy,
  A sargent thried and thrue,

It 's joost a daycent house I 'll build
  And rint it chape to you.
We 'll have a parlor, bedroom, hall,
  A duck-pond nately done,
With kitchen, pig-pen, praty-patch,
  And garret — all in one.

But, murther! there 's a baste, Biddy,
  That 's crapein' round a tree,
And well I know the crayture 's there
  To have a shot at me.
Now, Misther Rebel, say yere prayers,
  And howld yer dirthy paw,
Here goes! — be jabers, Biddy dear,
  I 've broke his oogly jaw!

THE IRISHMAN'S CHRISTMAS.

OLD Mother Earth makes Irishmen her universal pride,
You 'll find them all about the world, and ev'rywhere beside;
And good Saint Peter up above is often feeling tired,
Because of sainted Irishmen applying to be hired.

Thus, being good and plentiful, 't is proper we should find
A spacious house stuck full of them where'er we have a mind,
And unto such an edifice our present tale will reach,
With sixty nice, convenient rooms — a family in each.

No matter where it stands at all; but this we 'll let you know,
It constitutes itself along a fashionable row;
And when a bill of "Rooms to let" salutes you passing by,
You see recorded under it, "No Naygurs need apply."

Now, Mr. Mike O'Mulligan and servant boarded here, —
At least, his wife at service spent a portion of the year, —

And when, attired in pipe and hod, he left his parlor
door,
You felt the country had a vote it did n't have before.

Not much was M. O'Mulligan to festive ways inclined;
For chiefly on affairs of State he bent his giant mind;
But just for relaxation's sake he 'd venture now and
then,
To lead a jig, or break a head, like other Irishmen.

Says Mrs. Mike O'Mulligan, when Christmas came,
said she:
"Suppose we give a little ball this avening after tea;
The entry-way is broad enough to dance a dozen pairs,
And thim that does n't wish to dance can sit upon the
stairs."

"And sure," said M. O'Mulligan, "I don't object to
that;
But mind ye ask the girls entire, and ev'ry mother's
Pat;
I 'd wish them all, both girls and boys, to look at me
and see,
That, though I 'm School Commissioner, I 'm noways
proud," says he.

The matter being settled thus, the guests were notified,
And none to the O'Mulligans their presences denied;
But all throughout the spacious house the colleens
went to fix,
And left the men to clane themselves and twirl their
bits of sticks.

'T was great to see O'Mulligan, when came the proper
hour,
Stand smiling in the entry-way, as blooming as a flow'r,
And hear him to each lady say, "Well now, upon me
sowl!
Ye look more like an angel than like any other fowl."

And first came Teddy Finnigan, in collar tall and wide,
With Norah B. O'Flannigan demurely by his side;
And Alderman O'Grocery, and Councilman Maginn,
And both the Miss Mulrooneys, and the widow'd Mrs.
Flynn.

The Rileys, and the Shaunesseys, and Murphys all
were there,
Both male and female creatures of the manly and the
fair;
And crowded was the entry-way to such a great degree
They had to take their collars off to get their breathing free.

O'Grady with his fiddle was the orchestra engaged,
He tuned it on the banisters, and then the music raged;
"Now face your partners ev'ry man, and kape your eyes
on me,
And don't be turning in your toes indacently," says he.

And when the dance began to warm, the house began
to shake,
The windows, too, like loosen'd teeth, began to snap
and break;

The stove-pipes took the ague fit, and clatter'd to the floors,
And all the knobs and keys and locks were shaken from the doors.

The very shingles on the roof commenced to rattle out:
The chimney-stacks, like drunken men, insanely reel'd about;
A Thomas cat upon the eaves was shaken from his feet,
And right and left the shutters fell into the startled street.

It chanced, as M. O'Mulligan was fixing something hot,
The spoon was shaken from his hand, as likewise was the pot;
The plaster from the ceiling, too, came raining on his head,
And like a railway-carriage danced the table, chairs, and bed.

He tore into the entry-way, and "Stop the jig!" says he:
"It 's shakin' down the house ye are, as any one can see";
But not a soul in all the swarm to dance at all forbore,
And thumping down their brogans came, like hammers on the floor.

And then the house began to sway and strain and groan and crack,
And all the stairs about the place fell crashing, front and back;

The very air was full of dust, and in the walls the rats
Forgot, in newer perils found, all terror of the cats.

Then swifter flew O'Grady's bow, and "Mike, me lad," he roar'd,
"They 'll dance until they have n't left your floor a single board;
It 's sperits that they are," says he, "and I 'm a sperit, too;
And sperit, Mike O'Mulligan, is what we 'll make of you!"

"And sure," said M. O'Mulligan, though turning rather pale,
"It 's quite a handsome ghost ye are, and fit for any jail:
But tell me what I 've done to you offinsive in the laste;
And if I don't atone for it, I 'm nothing but a baste."

"It 's faithless to Saint Tammany ye are," O'Grady cried, —
And wilder, madder, grew the jig as he the fiddle plied, —
"It 's faithless to Saint Tammany, who bids the Irishman
Attain the highest office in this country that he can."

"Och hone!" says poor O'Mulligan, "it 's pretty well I 've done,
To be a School-Commissioner before I 'm thirty-one;

'T is barely just a year to-day since I set out from
Cork,
And now, be jabers! don't I hold an office in New
York?"

"Why, true for you, O'Mulligan," O'Grady roar'd
again;
"But what 's a School-Commissioner to what ye should
have been?
It 's Congressman, the very laste, an Irishman should
be,
And, since you 're not, receive the curse of Good Saint
Tammany!"

Then wilder danced the spirit crew, the fiddler gave a
scowl;
And scarce could fated Michael raise a good old Irish
howl,
When all the timbers in the house went tumbling with
a crash,
Reducing M. O'Mulligan to bits as small as hash!

Take warning now, all Irishmen, of what may be your
fate,
If you come home on Christmas night an hour or so
too late;
For sleeping on the garret stairs, and rolling down,
may be
To you, as unto Mike, a dream of good Saint Tammany!

THE IRISH EDITOR.

ME masculine parent was reared in Weehawken,
The merchant who hired him was Timothy Dod;
Of all the young clerks there was none like me father,
For he was the salesman that carried the hod.

One day he was flying right up a shteep ladder,
With plinty of bricks in his hod and his hat;
And joost as he shifted his foot for a second,
A rung it gave way, and me parent fell flat.

They sint for a coroner's jury and dochtor,
The last was too late and the former was not;
An inquest was held and a verdict was given —
'T was: "Death from a sun-sthroke of whiskey too hot."

And thus was I left for a swate little orphan,
Joost twenty years old, and with niver a cent;
Surrounded by those whose intintion was only
To trate me with grace till me fortune was spent.

'T was lucky I had such a fine education,
By raisin of making the fires for a school;

I wrote a large hand, and spoke Greek like a Hebrew—
  At laste I was towld so by Terence O'Toole.

So, what do I start but a newspaper spacious,
  And called it the "Irishman's Morning Gazette";
Got paper, and printing, and "items" on credit,
  And talked of the sheet to whomever I met.

Ah, sure! but a mighty nate thing I made of it:
  I towld of great doings before they occurr'd;
I got up fresh murders for each of me issues,
  And blackguarded all that I counted absurd.

I went into politics up to the handle,
  And proved that the country was ruin'd indade;
I called the postmasther a tief and a scoundrel,
  And eulogized freedom, free lunch, and free trade.

I trated of things that were doing in Europe,
  And wrote editorials all about kings;
I got up an illigant fancy news item
  About a strange pig that was throubled with wings.

I publish'd the essays of patent quack dochtors,
  I criticised actors, and pictures, and books;
And when a philanthropist paid his subscription,
  I spoke of "the affable Mr. ——'s good looks."

Och, murther! but did n't I lather the spalpeen
  That vainly pretinded to edit the "News";
I call'd him a mane, egotistical twaddler,
  Not worth the tobacco a gintleman chews.

Ah, sure, 't was a gintleman's paper I made it,—
  That dignified journal, the "Morning Gazette";
And nothing was wanting to finish me fortune,
  But all the subscribers I had n't got yet.

One morning, however, me giant edition
  Was taken as quick as it came from the press;
The person who took it was known as the sheriff,
  And what was the raisin I lave you to guess.

Thenceforth I retired from the footstool of gaynius,
  To mercantile life in the service of Dod;
And now, like me father, I'm simply yours truly,
  The clerk that makes mortar and carries the hod.

SONGS OF THE PERIOD.

"GIVE MY BOX-AND-STRING TO BROTHER."

(The American Boy's Very Last Request.)

GIVE my Box-and-String to Brother,
  Mamma, when I 'm dead ;
When the sexton puts me, mother,
  " In my little bed."
If the job is like to throw him,
  When the string he jerks,
Let him get some boy to show him
  How the old thing works.

Tell our neighbor that the tin hen,
  Causing all his rips,
Did n't finally cave-in when
  I "pass'd-in my chips" ;
Though your son forgives him, few know
  How he fired a shelf
Full of things to stop my — "you know
  How it is yourself."

Once he took to bootjack chucking
  From his room, when I

Ask'd him, while I made the clucking,
" How is that for high?"
If my fever ain't a sell, I 'll
Pardon spread on slim;
But if ever I get well, I 'll
" Put a head on him!"

"DEAR FATHER, LOOK UP."

(*Illustrative of American domestic Discipline and paternal Veracity.*)

DEAR Father, look up,
Away from the cup,
And tell me what aileth ma's forehead.
It 's all black-and-blue;
O, what could she do
To cause a contusion so horrid?

" Your mother, Jane Ann,
A newspaper man
Admired, till I warn'd her she 'd catch it;
Like Washington, I
Cannot tell a lie —
I did it with my little hatchet."

"WHEN YOUR CHEAP DIVORCE IS GRANTED."

(*From a Child in the Eastern States to her mother, temporarily absent from Home on a supposed visit to relatives in the West.*)

WHEN your cheap divorce is granted,
Mother, and you leave the West,
Shall I stay with you or father?
Tell me, mother, which the best?
He 'll be much surprised, I fear me,
When he knows what you have filed,
And, unless you hover near me,
He 'll appropriate your child.

Mother, if the move was needful;
If the income you and he
Shared so long, at last has bred an
Incompatibility;
If you 'll be his wife no longer,
When returning from the West,
Which am I to love the stronger?
Tell me, mother, which the best?

"O, BE NOT TOO HASTY, MY DEAREST."

(*Descriptive of a Morning-Call between fashionable sisters-in-law; as suggested by what the American "Round Table" and the English "Saturday Review" have revealed concerning the most respectable Women of Society.*)

O, BE not too hasty, my dearest,
  That cloth o'er the flagon to draw,
But pour in the goblet that 's nearest
  A swig for your sister-in-law.
I know that I 've taken already
  As much as beginner should stand;
But soda at home will soon steady
  The tremulous nerves of my hand.

"Pour out for yourself, my dear Bella,
  A couple of fingers, or so;
And don't you be getting too 'meller,'
  If home you have early to go.
Already the tint of our noses
  The pace is betraying, my dear;
And, after we 've taken our doses,
  Suppose we swear off, for a year."

"WHILE VIEWING THIS MENAGERIE."

(An American Sire and Son recognize and apply the Darwinian Moral of a popular Zoölogical Exhibition.)

WHILE viewing this menagerie,
  If smiles you 'd from your pa win,
I 'd have you bear in mind, my son,
  The works of Mr. Darwin ;
When yonder creature reaches for
  Your treasured candy-chunk, he
Exhibits such a hand as wore
  Our own ancestral monkey.

So do not mock at him, my child,
  Nor in your spirit jeer him,
But show a filial reverence
  Whenever you are near him.
Selection — Evolution — they
  In distance being sunk, he
Would be exactly like yourself,
  And you yourself a monkey.

" I 'll heed your lesson, dear papa,
  And treat the creature kindly,
And look on him —(as he on us,
  It 's likely) — not so blindly ;

For who can tell but that in turn,
  While staring from his bunk, he
Thinks you 're a cynocephalus,
  And I 'm your little monkey!"

THE END.

Cambridge: Electrotyped and Printed by Welch, Bigelow & Co

www.ingramcontent.com/pod-product-compliance
Lightning Source LLC
LaVergne TN
LVHW010236110826
845151LV00004B/1314

* 9 7 8 1 4 2 5 5 2 4 7 8 4 *